# Deliciously
## DAIRY FREE

hamlyn

# Deliciously
## DAIRY FREE

FRESH AND SIMPLE LACTOSE-FREE RECIPES
FOR HEALTHY EATING EVERY DAY

**Lesley Waters**

hamlyn

# Contents

# Introduction

Millions of people are affected by lactose intolerance, and many others these days simply prefer to avoid dairy products. When we first opened the doors of our cookery school in Dorset, England, ten years ago, we would receive the occasional request for dairy- or gluten-free options, but as time has gone by, we have seen major changes in what our students want: the courses offering healthier choices and those catering for more specialized dietary needs are growing in popularity. More and more people are waking up to the fact that healthy eating is not about "diet foods" but a really positive way of taking care of yourself and your family. *Deliciously Dairy Free* proposes a modern, lighter, and cleaner way of eating—a way of combining great ingredients with a simple, dairy-free approach.

I have always been interested in healthy eating, but I first got involved in dairy-free cooking when my mum was diagnosed with colitis years ago and needed to change her diet as a result. Back then, it was still difficult to find products that could be used in place of milk, cream, or cheese, but this has changed, with major supermarkets and health food stores now all stocking a good range of tasty alternatives. *Deliciously Dairy Free* will show you how to have fun and success in the kitchen without feeling that you are missing out.

We start off with a range of recipes that are perfect for breakfast and brunch, some of which also make quick snacks or appetizers ... real fast food, but fresh! The "Big Salads & Super Soups" in chapter 2 are meals in themselves: simple and satisfying, they really hit the spot. "Weekday Favorites" features speedy and delicious home-cooked suppers for family and friends: you'll find here cheats and swaps for all those favorite dishes you think are off limits, like Mac & Cheese, Spaghetti Carbonara, Creamy Chicken Curry, Pizza, and Classic Quiche. "Weekend Delights" covers spreads designed to impress your guests: you'll find appetizers, main courses, and special weekend food to be enjoyed indoors or alfresco. Proving that you can have your cake and eat it, "The Clean Bake" covers scrumptious cookies, pastries, and breads, while "Desserts" offers a selection of dairy-free desserts, including Raspberry & Banana Instant Ice Cream, Mega Saucy Chocolate Pud & Homemade Custard Sauce. Finally, "Basics" brings together a few staples of the dairy-free kitchen, from Cashew Honey Cream and DIY Fresh Almond Milk to a variety of stocks, sauces, and dressings that will add kick and a real edge to your dishes.

So, whether you suffer from lactose intolerance or you would simply prefer to ditch the dairy, this book will show you how easy it can be to transform the way you cook and eat by making only a few small changes. While writing, testing, and cooking the recipes in *Deliciously Dairy Free*, I realized that the dairy-free way of life is not about missing out—it's quite the opposite. This book is all about great-tasting, mouth-watering food for all occasions that everyone can enjoy!

# Recipe Finder

## Breakfast & Brunch

| Recipe | Page | Contains no eggs | Contains no nuts | Gluten/wheat-free | Vegetarian | Vegan |
|---|---|---|---|---|---|---|
| Banana & Peanut Butter Smoothie | 12 | • |  | • | • | • |
| Strawberry & Vanilla Cream Shake | 12 | • | • | • | • | • |
| Cinnamon & Vanilla French Toasts | 15 |  |  |  | • |  |
| Banana & Coconut Popover Pancakes with Maple & Lime | 16 |  | • |  | • |  |
| Scrambled Eggs with Pesto Toasts | 19 |  | • |  |  |  |
| Chilied Eggs on Scallion Rice | 20 |  | • | • | • |  |
| Brunch Bread & Chorizo Omelet | 22 |  | • |  |  |  |
| Hot Chili Baked Tomatoes | 22 | • | • | • |  |  |
| Pan Bagne | 23 | • | • |  |  |  |
| Beet Vodka Shots | 25 | • | • | • |  |  |
| Breakfast Bacon Popcorn | 25 | • | • | • |  |  |
| Mexican Corn Cakes with Avocado Crush | 26 |  | • |  | • |  |
| Spiked Balsamic Beefsteak Tomatoes | 29 |  | • |  |  |  |

## Big Salads & Super Soups

| Recipe | Page | Contains no eggs | Contains no nuts | Gluten/wheat-free | Vegetarian | Vegan |
|---|---|---|---|---|---|---|
| Tuscan Bread & Tomato Salad with Sweet Peppers & Black Olives | 32 | • | • |  |  |  |
| Broccoli Coleslaw | 34 | • | • | • | • | • |
| Asparagus with Tomato & Pea Dressing | 34 | • | • |  | • |  |
| Bacon & Croute Salad with Chile & Leek Poached Egg | 35 |  | • |  |  |  |
| Chunky Fries Salad with Ham Hock & Puy Lentil Dressing | 37 | • | • |  |  |  |
| Noodle Salad with Crispy Duck Legs | 38 |  | • |  |  |  |
| Pineapple & Smoked Chicken Sambal | 41 | • |  | • |  |  |
| Niçoise Rustic Board | 42 | • | • |  |  |  |
| Purple Sprouting Broccoli Soup with Tapenade Croutes | 45 | • | • |  | • |  |
| Parsnip & Chile Soup with Cardamom Crumbs | 46 | • |  |  |  |  |
| Thai Broth with Crispy Noodles | 47 | • |  |  |  |  |
| Spiced Sweet Potato Chowder | 48 | • | • | • | • |  |
| Barley Minestrone | 51 | • | • |  | • |  |
| Creamy Corn & Haddock Chowder | 52 | • | • | • |  |  |
| Pea & Bacon Chowder | 55 | • | • | • |  |  |
| Skillet Scones | 55 |  |  |  | • | • |

## Weekday Favorites

| Recipe | Page | Contains no eggs | Contains no nuts | Gluten/wheat-free | Vegetarian | Vegan |
|---|---|---|---|---|---|---|
| Pan-fried Vegetable Bhaji with Eggs & Wilted Greens | 58 |  | • | • | • |  |
| White Bean Creamy Hummus with Fava Bean Salad & Dukkah | 60 | • |  |  |  |  |
| Basil & Bean Linguine with Crispy Crumbs | 61 | • | • |  | • |  |
| Altogether Pasta Pronto | 63 | • | • |  | • | • |
| Double-baked Mac & Cheese with Roasted Vine Tomatoes | 64 | • | • |  |  |  |
| Summer Fresh Pea & Dried Tomato Risotto | 67 | • | • |  | • |  |
| Mushroom Stroganoff with Walnuts & Arugula | 68 | • |  |  |  |  |
| Welsh Rarebit Melts | 70 | • |  |  |  |  |
| Pasta Paella with Basil Ink | 71 | • |  |  |  |  |
| Fish Cachets | 72 | • |  |  |  |  |
| Creamy Garlic Mash | 73 | • | • | • | • | • |
| Creamy Lemon Potatoes with Herby Salmon | 75 | • |  |  |  |  |
| Fiery Fish Pie | 76 | • | • |  |  |  |
| Cracked Coriander Grilled Mackerel Fillets with Lentils | 77 | • | • |  |  |  |
| Garlic & Thyme Chicken with Cannellini & Potato Mash | 78 | • | • |  |  |  |
| Chorizo-crusted Chicken with Apple & Sage Cassoulet | 81 | • | • |  |  |  |
| Smoky Quesadilla Melts with Chicken, Cilantro & Avocado | 82 |  | • |  |  |  |
| Sesame Chicken Lickin' | 85 | • | • |  |  |  |
| Creamy Chicken Curry | 86 | • | • |  |  |  |
| Spaghetti alla Carbonara | 89 |  | • |  |  |  |
| Pizza Pizza Pizza | 90 | • | • |  |  |  |
| Classic Quiche | 93 |  | • |  |  |  |
| Roasted Cauliflower & Broccoli Mornay with a Chorizo Crumb | 94 | • | • |  |  |  |
| Luxury Beef & Prosciutto Lasagna with a Cheesy Nutmeg Sauce | 97 | • | • |  |  |  |
| Boston Bean Bake Topped with Olive Oil & Herb Dumplings | 98 | • | • |  |  |  |
| Soft Beef Kofta Meatballs in Sticky Glaze | 101 |  | • |  |  |  |
| Nutty Noodles with Wilted Greens & Sticky Beef | 102 |  | • |  |  |  |
| Pork & Prune Medallions with Creamy Cider & Mustard Sauce | 103 | • | • | • |  |  |

## Weekend Delights

| | Page | Contains no eggs | Contains no nuts | Gluten/wheat-free | Vegetarian | Vegan |
|---|---|---|---|---|---|---|
| Melon, Ham & Pine Nut Salad | 106 | • | | • | | |
| Asparagus with Watercress & Candied Walnut Salad | 109 | | | • | • | • |
| Vintage Egg Mayo with Tapenade & Cress | 110 | | • | • | | |
| Smoked Trout Bruschetta with Orange & Dill Relish | 113 | • | • | | | |
| Hot-smoked Salmon Horseradish Crème with Fresh Spinach Sauce | 114 | • | • | | | |
| Roasted Salt & Pepper Pears & Serrano Platter | 117 | • | • | | | |
| Duck with Warm Pomegranate, Puy Lentil & Orange Salad | 118 | • | • | • | | |
| Potato & Celeriac Pie with Canola Crust | 121 | | | | • | • |
| Crab & Ginger Tart with Soy-chili Dressing | 122 | | • | | | |
| Chicken Tagine with Red Lentils & Rice | 125 | • | • | • | | |
| Saffron-baked Orange Poussin with Crispy-topped Risotto | 126 | • | • | | | |
| Roasted Guinea Fowl with Cardamom Bread Sauce | 127 | • | | | | |
| Slow-cooked Lamb with Lemon & Oregano | 128 | • | • | • | | |
| Salt & Thyme Crusted Pork Belly | 130 | • | • | • | | |
| Rich Steak & Venison Pie with a Black Pepper Crust | 131 | | • | | | |
| Hot Black Bean Sweet Chunky Chili with Steak Burgers & Skinny Fries | 133 | • | • | • | | |

## The Clean Bake

| | Page | Contains no eggs | Contains no nuts | Gluten/wheat-free | Vegetarian | Vegan |
|---|---|---|---|---|---|---|
| Caramelized Onion & Spelt Flatbread | 137 | • | • | | • | |
| Focaccia with Rosemary | 138 | • | • | | • | |
| Thyme, Garlic & Chile Socca | 139 | • | • | • | • | |
| Cracked Black Pepper & Figgy Bread | 140 | • | • | | • | |
| Bacon & Sage Cornbread | 142 | • | | | | |
| Cheese & Chive Soda Bread | 142 | • | | | • | |
| Poppy Seed Grissini | 143 | • | • | | | |
| Vanilla Bean & Olive Oil Layer Cake | 145 | | • | | • | |
| Carrot & Walnut Muffelettas | 146 | | • | | • | |
| Lime Chocolate Cupcakes with Chili Fondant Sauce | 147 | | | | • | |
| Cinnamon & Orange Cookies | 148 | • | • | | • | • |
| Cocoa Crumble Cookies | 148 | • | • | | • | • |
| Coconut & Lime Cake | 150 | | • | • | • | |

## Desserts

| | Page | Contains no eggs | Contains no nuts | Gluten/wheat-free | Vegetarian | Vegan |
|---|---|---|---|---|---|---|
| Salted Caramel Banana Toffee Tatin | 154 | • | • | | • | |
| Coconut Rice Pudding with Grilled Pineapple | 156 | • | • | • | • | |
| Summer Pudding Jam | 157 | • | • | • | • | |
| Rhubarb & Vanilla Jam | 157 | • | • | • | • | |
| Roasted Vanilla Nectarines with Sweet Wine & Berry Sauce | 159 | • | • | • | • | |
| Meringue Nougats | 159 | | • | • | • | |
| Plummy Chocolate Mousse with Pistachios | 160 | | • | • | | |
| Rhubarb, Almond & Orange Pudding Cake | 163 | | • | • | | |
| Mega Saucy Chocolate Pud with Orange Coconut Cream | 164 | | • | | • | |
| Raspberry & Banana Instant Ice Cream | 167 | • | • | | • | |
| Cider Baked Apple Pie with Cornmeal Pastry | 168 | | • | | • | |
| Homemade Custard Sauce | 169 | | • | | • | |
| Frangipane Plum Tart | 170 | | | | • | |
| Lemon Posset with Strawberries | 171 | • | • | • | • | |
| Sparkling Jellies | 171 | • | • | • | • | |
| Chocolate Cornmeal Cake with Espresso Syrup | 172 | | | • | • | |
| Chocolate & Apricot Fudgy Refrigerator Cake | 175 | • | • | | • | |

## Basics

| | Page | Contains no eggs | Contains no nuts | Gluten/wheat-free | Vegetarian | Vegan |
|---|---|---|---|---|---|---|
| DIY Fresh Almond Milk | 177 | • | | • | • | • |
| Cashew Honey Cream | 178 | • | | • | • | |
| Instant Peanut Butter | 178 | • | | • | • | |
| Hazelnut Chocolate Spread | 179 | • | | • | • | |
| Cranberry, Red Cabbage & Juniper Jam | 180 | • | • | • | • | • |
| Roast Tomato Chutney | 181 | • | • | • | • | |
| Sweet Pepper Chutney | 181 | • | • | • | • | |
| Honey, Mustard & Cider Vinaigrette | 182 | • | • | • | | |
| Warm Ginger & Orange Sesame Dressing | 182 | • | • | • | • | • |
| Soured Cream & Tarragon Dressing | 183 | • | • | • | • | |
| Smoked Pepper Rouille | 183 | • | • | | • | |
| Classic Pesto | 184 | • | | • | • | |
| Fava Bean & Basil Pistou | 184 | • | • | | • | |
| Smoked Garlic & Chive Mayo | 185 | | • | • | • | |
| Curry Gravy | 185 | • | • | | • | |
| Citrus Chicken Stock Pot | 186 | • | • | • | | |
| Bouquet Garni Stock | 187 | • | • | • | • | • |

# Breakfast
# & Brunch

*My daughter Scout loves this Banana & Peanut Butter Smoothie…*
*rich, thick and creamy, like a diner-style milkshake. If you want*
*it thinner, simply add a little more dairy-free milk or ice cubes.*
*The Strawberry & Vanilla Cream Shake (below) is a classic*
*combination of flavors. Make sure you use sweet, ripe strawberries,*
*but when not in season, frozen berries are a good alternative. For*
*an adult twist, I love to finish each glass with*
*a small grinding of black pepper. This is extra delicious*
*served with the Cocoa Crumble Cookies (see page 148).*

# Banana & Peanut Butter Smoothie

### MAKES 4 SMALL GLASSES
### OR 2 LARGE GLASSES

2 small bananas

3 tablespoons Instant Peanut Butter
(see page 178)

6 ice cubes

1¼ cups hazelnut, almond
(see page 177 for homemade),
or soy milk

Place everything in a blender and blend until really smooth.

Serve straight away.

# Strawberry & Vanilla Cream Shake

### MAKES 4 MEDIUM-SIZE GLASSES

2 cups ripe strawberries, hulled

2 teaspoons vanilla bean paste

1 cup soy, oat, or almond milk (see
page 177 for homemade)

3 tablespoons dairy-free light cream

ice, to serve

Place all the ingredients in a blender and blend until creamy and smooth.

Half-fill 4 medium-size glasses with ice and pour over the shake. Serve straight away.

*A little bit of indulgence in the morning goes a long way—simply swap in some dairy-free milk for a delicious start to your day.*

# Cinnamon & Vanilla French Toasts with Bananas, Strawberries & Maple Syrup

### SERVES 4

3 free-range eggs

1¼ cups almond (see page 177 for homemade) or hazelnut milk

1 teaspoon ground cinnamon

1 teaspoon good-quality vanilla extract

canola oil, for frying

½ dairy-free fruit or fig loaf, sliced into 8

sifted confectioners' sugar, for dusting (optional)

2 bananas, cut into chunky slices

8 large strawberries, hulled and cut into quarters

maple syrup, to serve

Beat together the eggs, milk, cinnamon, and vanilla in a bowl.

Place a large, nonstick skillet over medium heat and add a splash of oil.

Dip the bread slices into the eggy mixture (not for too long or the bread will become soggy) and fry, in batches, for about 2 minutes each side or until golden brown and puffy. Remove from pan and keep warm in a low oven while you finish cooking all the toasts.

To serve, place 2 slices of French toast on each warmed serving plate and dust with confectioners' sugar, if desired. Top with the bananas, strawberries, and a good drizzle of maple syrup.

*You can now buy fresh coconut milk from the chiller section in many supermarkets. However, you can use canned coconut milk or even almond (see page 177 for a DIY version) or hazelnut milk if you prefer. Ring the changes by using sliced strawberries or peaches instead of bananas.*

# Banana & Coconut Popover Pancakes with Maple & Lime

### SERVES 4

2 free-range eggs

2 tablespoons granulated sugar

1½ cups all-purpose flour

1 tablespoon baking powder

⅓ cup unsweetened shredded coconut, plus extra for sprinkling

generous 1 cup coconut milk

sunflower oil, for frying

3 bananas, sliced

TO SERVE

maple syrup

lime wedges, for squeezing over

Beat together the eggs and sugar in a bowl. Mix in the flour, baking powder, and shredded coconut, then beat in the coconut milk until you have a smooth batter.

Heat a little oil in a large, nonstick skillet. Ladle in the mixture —you will probably be able to cook the batter in batches of 2 or 3. Cook over medium heat until small bubbles appear on the surface of the batter, then arrange slices of banana over the top of each and sprinkle with a little extra coconut. Cook for another 1–2 minutes or until golden on the underside and firm enough to flip over.

Carefully flip the pancakes over and cook for 1–2 minutes more or until just firm and golden. Flip onto a plate and keep warm in a low oven while you cook the remaining batter.

Serve piled up, drizzled with maple syrup and a squeeze of lime juice.

*There is nothing more comforting than creamy scrambled eggs, and it's a real treat when combined with pesto and smothered on sourdough toasts. My favorite version is with the addition of smoked salmon or trout, whereas my husband likes his topped with very crispy bacon.*

# Scrambled Eggs with Pesto Toasts

### SERVES 4

10 free-range eggs

2 tablespoons dairy-free light cream

4 large slices of dairy-free sourdough bread

1 tablespoon olive oil

5 tablespoons Classic Pesto (see page 184)

salt and pepper

Break the eggs into a bowl and use a fork to blend them, then gently beat in the cream and salt and pepper. Put the bread on to toast.

Pour the oil into a medium-size, heavy nonstick saucepan and place over medium heat. Add the egg mixture to the pan and, using a wooden spoon, start stirring briskly back and forth, getting into the corner of the pan and keeping the eggs moving all the time.

Once three-quarters of the egg is creamy and firm and the rest liquid, remove the pan from the heat. Keep on stirring but do not return to the heat—the eggs will cook in the residual heat of the pan.

To serve, spread the toast with a thick layer of the pesto. Top with the creamy scrambled eggs and serve straight away.

*I first had these steamed eggs with an Asian twist in Thailand,*
*and they are a great hangover cure! It's now a family favorite,*
*not only for breakfast but for any time of day.*

# Chilied Eggs on Scallion Rice

### SERVES 2

¾ cup basmati rice, washed

2 tablespoons canola oil

1 bunch of scallions, coarsely chopped

2 large free-range eggs

2 tablespoons cilantro leaves

1 red chile, seeded and cut into slivers

salt and pepper

Tabasco sauce or chili ketchup, to serve

Cook the basmati rice according to the package instructions, then drain well if necessary.

Heat 1 tablespoon of the oil in a nonstick skillet, add the scallions and fry for 3–4 minutes, until golden and soft. Stir into the cooked rice, season to taste with salt and pepper and set to one side.

Heat the remaining oil in the skillet and crack in the eggs.

Sprinkle the eggs with the cilantro leaves and chile, and season well with salt and pepper. Cover the pan with a tight-fitting lid and allow the eggs to gently steam until just cooked.

To serve, place a dome of scallion rice in the center of 2 large, warmed plates. Top each with an egg and shake over Tabasco or chili ketchup.

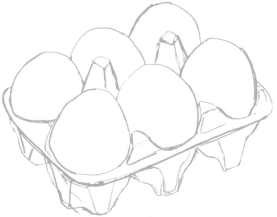

*In this take on a Spanish tortilla, pieces of fried bread are used instead of potatoes. This omelet is great served with spinach salad and Roast Tomato Chutney (see page 181). The Hot Chili Baked Tomatoes (below) go wonderfully with the Mexican Corn Cakes (see page 26), and are great as part of a mezze platter.*

# Brunch Bread & Chorizo Omelet

## SERVES 4

1 tablespoon olive oil

3oz cured chorizo sausage, chopped

2 thick slices of dairy-free sourdough bread or focaccia, coarsely chopped

6 free-range eggs

⅓ cup finely grated dairy-free cheddar-style cheese

salt and pepper

Preheat the broiler to medium.

Heat the oil in a medium-size, nonstick skillet, add the chorizo and fry over medium heat for 2 minutes. Add the bread, stir to mix well and cook for 2–3 minutes or until golden and crisp.

Break the eggs into a bowl, beat together and season well.

Pour the eggs into the pan and cook for 2–3 minutes. Sprinkle over the cheese.

Place the pan under the broiler for 2–3 minutes, until the omelet is just set, golden, and bubbling.

---

# Hot Chili Baked Tomatoes

## SERVES 4

8 ripe vine tomatoes, separated from the vine but with the stalks left on

6oz slices of air-cured ham

2 tablespoons virgin olive oil

2 teaspoons sugar

2 large mild red chiles, seeded and finely diced

Preheat the oven to 400°F.

Cut a small slice from the base of each tomato to allow them to stand upright.

Lay out the slices of air-cured ham, drizzle with the olive oil and sprinkle with the sugar and chiles. Carefully wrap each tomato in a slice of coated ham and place on a baking sheet.

Bake the wrapped tomatoes for 15–20 minutes, until they are soft but still holding their shape and the ham is crisp.

*This is my simplified version of a traditional Mediterranean sandwich. It's perfect for outdoor brunch and it's also great for picnics, as it travels really well. You need to make this the day before to allow all the flavors to infuse and soak into the bread. I always bring along a little jar of extra balsamic vinegar and olive oil to drizzle over once the pan bagne is cut into thick wedges.*

# Pan Bagne

### SERVES 6

¼ cup balsamic vinegar

1 garlic clove, crushed

7 tablespoons extra virgin olive oil

1 round, flat dairy-free whole-grain or sourdough loaf, about 13oz

salt and pepper

### FILLING

9½ oz semidried tomatoes in oil, drained and roughly chopped

7½ oz antipasti artichokes in oil, drained and coarsely sliced

24 black olives, pitted

7½ oz antipasti roasted peppers in oil, drained and coarsely sliced

3 tablespoons baby capers, drained

1 large ripe avocado, halved, pitted, peeled, and sliced

1 small bunch of basil leaves

For the dressing, mix together the balsamic vinegar, garlic, and oil in a small bowl and season to taste with salt and pepper.

Slice the loaf horizontally into 3 layers.

Generously sprinkle each layer with the dressing. Set the top of the loaf to one side.

Sprinkle the bottom and middle layers of bread with the filling ingredients. Drizzle over the remaining dressing and reassemble the loaf.

Press the layers together well and wrap the loaf tightly in plastic wrap. Place on a large plate and top with another 2–3 plates to help compress the loaf. Chill overnight before serving.

To serve, unwrap, place on a board and cut in half to reveal the filling. Using a large, serrated bread knife, carefully cut each half into thick wedges.

*You don't need a juicer to make Beet Vodka Shots—there are some fabulous beet juices available. Make as spicy as you dare and serve over plenty of ice. This also works really well with gin. Serve with smoked salmon on rye toasts or Breakfast Bacon Popcorn (see below), which is easy to cook, fun to serve, and incredibly moreish. Once the corn starts to pop, don't lift the lid—it's done when the popping sound stops.*

# Beet Vodka Shots

### SERVES 4

1¼ cups vodka

3¾ cups beet juice

a few shakes of Tabasco sauce, or to taste

1 teaspoon celery salt

4 celery sticks

4 lime wedges

ice, to serve

Mix together the vodka, beet juice, Tabasco, and celery salt in a large pitcher.

Pour into 4 tumblers half-filled with ice. Finish each glass with a celery stick and a lime wedge.

---

# Breakfast Bacon Popcorn

### SERVES 6

2 tablespoons sunflower oil

4oz smoked bacon lardons

2 tablespoons chopped rosemary

½ cup popping corn

Heat the oil in a large saucepan with a tight-fitting lid. Stir in the bacon lardons and cook for 3 minutes or until golden. Stir in half the rosemary.

Remove the pan from the heat, add the popcorn kernels and cover with the lid. Place the pan back over medium heat for 2–3 minutes. You will start to hear the corn pop loudly. Shake the pan occasionally until the sound of corn popping has stopped.

Stir in the remaining rosemary and pour out into a serving bowl. Serve straight away.

*These scrummy corn cakes topped with a creamy avocado crush make a feast of Mexican and Mediterranean flavors when served with Hot Chili Baked Tomatoes (see page 22). I like to add warm taco chips on the side too.*

# Mexican Corn Cakes with Avocado Crush

### SERVES 4

¾ cup all-purpose flour

1¾ teaspoons baking powder

1 cup drained canned corn kernels in water

2 large free-range eggs, beaten

⅔ cup dairy-free milk

2 tablespoons olive oil

pepper

AVOCADO CRUSH

2 ripe avocados, halved, pitted, peeled, and cut into small chunks

juice of 1 lime

1 garlic clove, crushed

2 shallots, finely chopped

8 cherry tomatoes, quartered

1 large red chile, seeded and finely chopped

2 tablespoons extra virgin olive oil

salt and pepper

To make the avocado crush, place the avocado in a bowl and squeeze over the lime juice. Gently mix in the other crush ingredients and season to taste with salt and pepper. Set to one side.

Sift together the flour and baking powder into a large bowl and season with a little pepper. Add the corn kernels, eggs, and milk and quickly mix together to form a loose batter.

Heat 1 tablespoon of the oil in a large, nonstick skillet. Spoon 3 heaps of the mixture into the pan and gently press out to form 3 rough thick rounds. Fry over medium heat for 2–3 minutes, until golden, then flip over and cook for another 1–2 minutes, until golden and cooked. Remove from the pan and keep warm in a low oven while you cook the remaining corn cakes.

To serve, pile the corn cakes on a board, then spoon the avocado crush into a serving bowl and place next to them.

*Breakfast with a zing—these sizzling tomatoes with an extra bite of chile and balsamic vinegar will soon get you going. If you can't face chile in the morning, try sprinkling the tomatoes with a little basil, or omit the balsamic and sprinkle over the more traditional Worcestershire sauce. Serve them my favorite way as below, with toasted dairy-free rye or sourdough bread and a poached egg.*

# Spiked Balsamic Beefsteak Tomatoes with Crispy Ham & Poached Egg

### SERVES 4

4 beefsteak tomatoes, halved

1 teaspoon dried red pepper flakes

1 teaspoon sugar

2 tablespoons olive oil

2¾oz slices of air-cured ham

pepper

#### TO SERVE

4 slices of dairy-free rye or sourdough bread

4 very fresh free-range eggs

1 tablespoon white wine vinegar

2 tablespoons balsamic vinegar

Preheat the oven to 400°F. Place the tomatoes cut side up on a baking sheet.

Mix together the red pepper flakes, sugar, and 1½ tablespoons of the oil in a bowl, then drizzle over the tomato halves. Grind over plenty of black pepper.

Bake for 12–15 minutes, until the tomatoes are cooked through but still keeping their shape.

Meanwhile, heat the remaining oil in a skillet over medium heat and fry the ham for about 1 minute on each side or until crispy. Toast the bread.

For the perfect poached egg, first start with really fresh eggs. Bring a shallow saucepan filled two-thirds with water to a simmer and add the white wine vinegar. Crack each egg into a small cup and gently tip into the lightly simmering water. Allow the eggs to settle and cook for about 2–3 minutes, until just set. They will eventually float to the top. Lift out the cooked eggs with a slotted spoon and rest the spoon briefly on paper towels to remove the excess water. Gently slide each poached egg onto a slice of toast on a warmed serving plate and season with pepper.

Divide the tomatoes among the plates and drizzle each with a little balsamic vinegar. Top with the crispy ham and serve straight away.

# Big
# Salads
# & Super
# Soups

*This summer salad is fab with canned tuna in olive oil, or if you want to be more extravagant, try it with fresh griddled tuna steaks. If fish isn't your thing, then serve it with griddled chicken or crispy air-cured ham.*

# Tuscan Bread & Tomato Salad with Sweet Peppers & Black Olives

### SERVES 4

4 thick slices of dairy-free sourdough bread or focaccia

3 tablespoons extra virgin olive oil, plus extra for drizzling

1 garlic clove, crushed

8oz baby plum tomatoes, halved

1 large red bell pepper, cored, seeded, and diced

½ cup mixed black and green olives, pitted and torn in half

2 tablespoons baby capers, drained and rinsed

1 small red onion, finely chopped

1 mild red chile, seeded and finely chopped

1 small bunch of basil

2 (4oz) cans good-quality tuna in olive oil, drained and flaked

salt and pepper

Preheat the oven to 425°F.

Tear the bread into large bite-size pieces and place in a bowl. Mix half the oil and garlic together and drizzle over the bread. Toss together until well coated.

Transfer the bread to a baking sheet and bake for 12–15 minutes or until golden and crisp.

Meanwhile, toss together the tomatoes, bell pepper, olives, capers, onion, chile, and remaining olive oil in a large bowl. Season well with salt and pepper.

Add the warm croutons to the tomato mixture with two-thirds of the basil and gently mix.

To serve, spoon the salad into a mound into the center of each serving bowl and top each with flakes of tuna, the remaining basil leaves, a drizzle of olive oil, and pepper.

*Coleslaw can be a sensational salad or side dish—delicious and crisp.
You will need really fresh broccoli here to make the grating easy.*

# Broccoli Coleslaw

### SERVES 6

1 head of broccoli, about 1lb

1 fennel bulb, trimmed and finely sliced

2 garlic cloves, crushed

1 large red onion, finely chopped

¼ cup dairy-free mayonnaise

juice of 1 lime

salt and pepper

Cut the broccoli into large florets, including some of the stalk. Shred on the large side of a hand grater and place in a bowl.

Add the fennel, garlic, and red onion to the shredded broccoli and mix together well.

Add the mayonnaise and lime juice and toss together, then season to taste with salt and pepper.

---

*It only takes a few minutes to put this colorful warm salad together.*

# Asparagus with Tomato & Pea Dressing

### SERVES 4

2 bunches of young asparagus, trimmed

¼ cup olive oil, plus extra for drizzling

1½ tablespoons cold water

8oz baby plum or cherry tomatoes, halved

⅔ cup frozen peas, defrosted

2 tablespoons balsamic vinegar

2 tablespoons pine nuts, toasted

pepper

Wash the asparagus and place the wet asparagus with half the oil in a bowl. Grind over some black pepper and toss together well.

Heat a large, nonstick skillet until hot, add the asparagus and fry for 2 minutes. Reduce the heat, then add the measured water, cover with a lid and cook for another 3–4 minutes or until the asparagus is just tender. Remove the asparagus from the pan and divide among 4 warmed serving plates.

Add the remaining oil to the skillet and increase the heat to high. Add the tomatoes to the pan and cook for 1 minute, then add the peas and cook for another 2 minutes or until heated through. Drizzle over the balsamic vinegar and shake the pan to coat the tomatoes.

Spoon the tomatoes and peas and any juices over the asparagus. Sprinkle with the pine nuts, drizzle over a little extra olive oil and grind over black pepper, then serve straight away with warm crusty bread.

*This delicious salad is so quick and easy to prepare. Toasting the bread keeps it crispy and adds a real crunch to the salad. The secret of this simple salad is to cook the poached egg until just soft so that it can ooze all over the dressed leaves.*

# Bacon & Croute Salad
# with Chile & Leek Poached Egg

### SERVES 4

2 large slices of rustic dairy-free bread, such as focaccia or sourdough

3 tablespoons extra virgin olive oil

1 leek, trimmed, cleaned, and very finely shredded into strips

1 red chile, seeded and cut into slivers

splash of balsamic vinegar

8 slices bacon

1 tablespoon white wine vinegar

4 very fresh free-range eggs

about 3 cups bag mixed salad greens

pepper

Preheat the oven to 400°F. Preheat the broiler to high.

Tear the bread into bite-size pieces and place in a bowl. Add half the oil and toss together until well coated.

Transfer the bread to a baking sheet and bake for 8 minutes or until golden and crisp.

Meanwhile, heat the remaining oil in a small saucepan. Add the leek and chile and gently fry for 1–2 minutes, until softened. Stir in the balsamic vinegar.

Broil the bacon for 5–6 minutes, until crispy, turning once.

For the poached eggs, bring a shallow saucepan filled two-thirds with water to a simmer and add the white wine vinegar. Crack each egg into a small cup and gently tip into the lightly simmering water. Allow the eggs to settle and cook for about 2–3 minutes, until just set. They will eventually float to the top. Lift out the cooked eggs with a slotted spoon and rest the spoon briefly on paper towels to remove the excess water.

To serve, transfer the leeks and chile to a large bowl and toss with the salad greens and crisp croutons. Divide among 4 serving plates. Top each plate with a poached egg and grind over a little black pepper. Top each serving with 2 pieces of crispy bacon and serve at once.

*Ham and fries gets poshed up with a zingy balsamic and lentil dressing. This dressing is also delicious served with grilled fish, seafood, or roast chicken or simply drizzled over roasted veggies. Don't be tempted to use canned lentils here, as they are too soft.*

# Chunky Fries Salad with Ham Hock & Puy Lentil Dressing

## SERVES 4

1¾ lb potatoes, washed but unpeeled

2 tablespoons olive oil

6oz cooked ham hock, flaked

2 cups pea shoots or mixed salad greens

1 quantity of Balsamic & Puy Lentil Dressing (see below)

salt and pepper

### BALSAMIC & PUY LENTIL DRESSING

3 tablespoons cooked Puy lentils

2 tablespoons balsamic vinegar

5 tablespoons extra virgin olive oil

1 garlic clove, crushed

4 sundried tomatoes in oil, drained and chopped

salt and pepper

Preheat the oven to 400°F. Line a roasting pan with parchment paper.

Trim the potatoes into squares and cut each into 1.5-cm (¾-inch) chunky fries.

Place the fries in the lined pan, add the oil and toss to coat. Season well with salt and pepper.

Bake for 35–40 minutes or until cooked through and golden.

Meanwhile, for the balsamic and puy lentil dressing, place all the ingredients in a small bowl and gently mix together. Season to taste with salt and pepper.

Toss the ham hock and pea shoots together and pile a mound on each serving plate. Top each with a pile of chunky fries and drizzle over the dressing.

*Add an interesting twist to noodles with a dressing of ginger, orange, and sesame. These fresh, sweet, and aromatic flavors just pop in the mouth. This salad is also great served with grilled salmon or tuna.*

# Noodle Salad with Crispy Duck Legs

## SERVES 4

4 duck legs

2 teaspoons sea salt

1 cup sugar snap peas

7oz medium egg noodles

1⅓ cups shredded collard greens

2 large carrots, peeled and then peeled into ribbons with a vegetable peeler

6 scallions, finely sliced

1 bunch of cilantro leaves

1 quantity of Warm Ginger & Orange Sesame Dressing (see page 182)

salt

Preheat the oven to 400°F.

Using a small, sharp knife, prick the duck legs all over. Place on a wire rack set over a roasting pan. Rub salt all over the duck legs and roast for about 45–50 minutes, until crispy and cooked through.

Meanwhile, cook the noodles according to the package instructions, then drain.

Blanch the sugar snap peas in a saucepan of boiling water for 1 minute, then drain and refresh under cold running water. Halve lengthwise.

Blanch and refresh the collard greens in the same way. Drain well.

Toss together the noodles, sugar snap peas, collard greens, carrots, scallions and half the cilantro leaves in a bowl. Add the warm dressing and toss to coat.

Once the duck is cooked, remove from the oven. To shred the duck, use 2 forks to remove the crispy skin and meat from each leg. Pile some noodle salad into each serving bowl, top with the crispy duck and sprinkle with the remaining cilantro. Serve straight away.

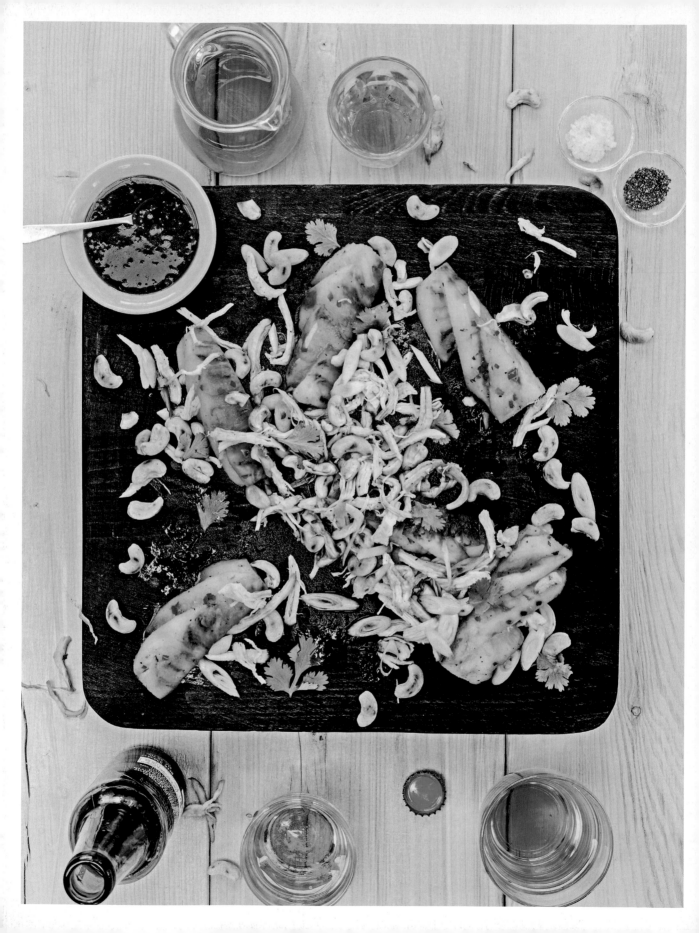

*If you've never had pineapple this way, you've got to try this recipe. It's a real showstopper—I love to present it as a huge rustic board, put it in the middle of the table and let everyone help themselves. You can use cold leftover chicken in place of the smoked, and the pineapple also makes a great dessert served with crumbly meringues and your favorite dairy-free ice cream or sorbet.*

# Pineapple & Smoked Chicken Sambal

### SERVES 4

1 large, sweet ripe pineapple

1 red chile, seeded and finely chopped

2 tablespoons honey

juice of 2 oranges

⅔ cup raw cashew nuts, toasted and chopped

4 scallions, finely chopped

2 tablespoons chopped cilantro

1 tablespoon extra virgin olive oil

5oz cooked smoked chicken, finely shredded

salt and pepper

Cut the top and bottom off the pineapple and cut away all the skin including the "eyes," then quarter and remove the core from each wedge. Cut each wedge in half, giving 8 wedges in total.

Place the pineapple wedges in a bowl and add the chile, honey, and orange juice. Toss well and set aside for 10 minutes to marinate.

Meanwhile, mix the cashew nuts, scallions, cilantro, and olive oil together in a bowl, season to taste with salt and pepper and set to one side.

Heat a ridged grill pan over medium heat. Remove the pineapple wedges from the marinade, reserving the marinade, and add to the pan. Cook for 2–3 minutes on each side or until lightly charred.

Arrange the pineapple on a large rustic board, then top with the chicken and sprinkle with the cashew nut relish.

Pour the reserved marinade into the hot grill pan and let it bubble off the heat for a few seconds until syrupy, then drizzle over the finished dish.

*Don't be put off by the long list of ingredients here. This salad can use any leftovers you have on hand—cold chicken, cold new potatoes, salami and air-cured meats, antipasti artichokes or eggplants, and any salad greens you fancy. Present it on a large rustic-style board for full effect, and it's great with the Soured Cream & Tarragon Dressing (see page 183) or the Smoked Garlic & Chive Mayo (see page 185). Traditionally this salad is served with potatoes and anchovy fillets too, but I prefer to serve it with the Caramelized Onion & Spelt Flatbread (see page 136) or the Thyme, Garlic & Chile Socca (see page 139).*

# Niçoise Rustic Board

### SERVES 6

2 cups green beans, topped and tailed

3 peppered smoked mackerel fillets, skinned

2 skinless smoked trout fillets

1 tablespoon balsamic vinegar

3 tablespoons extra virgin olive oil

1 small red onion, finely chopped

3 large ripe plum tomatoes, coarsely chopped

2 heads of white or red endive, each cut into 4 wedges

1 (11½oz) jar antipasti roasted peppers in oil, drained

1⅓ cups mixed olives

3 cups frisée (curly chicory) leaves

4 free-range eggs, hard-cooked, shelled and halved

salt and pepper

Cook the green beans in a saucepan of boiling water for 3–4 minutes until just tender, then drain, refresh under cold water and pat dry. Set to one side.

Pull the fish into large flakes and set to one side.

Mix the balsamic vinegar, olive oil, and red onion together in a small bowl. Season well with salt and pepper.

Place the green beans and tomatoes separately in small bowls. Divide the dressing between each and toss well. Set to one side.

Arrange the flaked fish, endive, peppers, olives, frisée, and egg halves in clusters on the board. Add the dressed green beans and tomatoes. Take to the table with the dressing of your choice and warm bread, and allow everyone to help themselves.

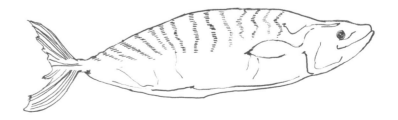

*I know it's not a chefy thing to admit, but give me purple sprouting broccoli in place of asparagus any day! This vibrant, hearty soup with Mediterranean crumbly croutes is a real taste sensation. If you have ardent meat lovers in the family, simply fry off a little chopped chorizo and sprinkle with the croutes.*

# Purple Sprouting Broccoli Soup with Tapenade Croutes

## SERVES 4

2 tablespoons olive oil

1 onion, finely chopped

1 red chile, kept whole

1lb purple sprouting broccoli, trimmed

1 cup frozen peas

4 cups hot vegetable stock

6 tablespoons dairy-free light cream

salt and pepper

### TAPENADE CROUTES

1 small dairy-free focaccia loaf, torn into bite-size pieces

extra virgin olive oil, for drizzling

12 green olives, pitted and chopped

1 small bunch of basil, leaves torn

Preheat the oven to 400°F.

Heat the oil in a saucepan, add the onion and cook gently for 5 minutes, until softened.

Add the chile, broccoli, peas, and hot stock and bring to a boil, then reduce the heat and simmer for 6 minutes.

Remove the chile from the soup, split in half and remove the seeds and stem. Transfer the soup to a blender with the chile and blend until smooth.

Return the soup to a clean pan and stir in the cream. Season to taste with salt and pepper and heat through gently.

Meanwhile, for the tapenade croutes, place the focaccia on a baking sheet, drizzle with olive oil and bake for 8 minutes or until golden and crisp.

Toss the toasted focaccia with the olives and torn basil leaves.

Ladle the soup into warmed serving bowls and top with the tapenade croutes. Drizzle with a little extra olive oil and serve straight away.

*This delicately spiced soup is really rich and creamy. But the thing that makes it extra special is the nutty topping of roasted cashews spiced with aromatic cardamom.*

# Parsnip & Chile Soup with Cardamom Crumbs

## SERVES 6

2 tablespoons olive oil

1 onion, chopped

1 small leek, trimmed, cleaned, and chopped

1 red chile, kept whole

1½lb parsnips, peeled and chopped

grated zest of 1 unwaxed lime

4 cups vegetable stock

2 tablespoons dairy-free light cream, plus extra, to serve (optional)

salt and pepper

### CRUMBS

2 tablespoons canola oil

7 cardamom pods, crushed and husks discarded

2½ cups dairy-free fresh white bread crumbs

¼ cup salted roasted cashew nuts, finely chopped

Heat the oil in a saucepan, add the onion, leek, and chile and cook gently for 5 minutes, until softened. Add the parsnips and lime zest, stir well and cook for 2 minutes.

Add the stock and bring to a boil, then reduce the heat and simmer for 15–20 minutes.

Remove the chile from the soup, split in half and remove the seeds and stem. Transfer the soup to a blender with the chile and blend until smooth.

Return the soup to a clean pan and stir in the cream, if using. Season to taste with salt and pepper and heat through gently.

To make the crumbs, heat the canola oil in a large, nonstick skillet, stir in the cardamom seeds and cook over medium heat for 30 seconds. Add the bread crumbs and cashews and fry, stirring frequently, for 5 minutes, until golden and crispy.

Serve the soup topped with the crispy crumbs and dairy-free cream, if desired.

*This broth has aromatic spice, heat, and freshness. Cauliflower is often seen as mundane, but teamed here with cashews, spinach, and spice, it's anything but. Use this Thai broth as a base for all Thai-style curries such as fish, shellfish, chicken, beef, or pork.*

# Thai Broth with Crispy Noodles

### SERVES 4

1⅔ cups canned coconut milk

1¼ cups vegetable stock

1½ cups cauliflower florets

sunflower oil, for deep-frying

4oz rice noodles

1 cup spinach, coarsely shredded

⅔ cup raw cashew nuts, toasted

cilantro leaves, for sprinkling

### CURRY PASTE

2 tablespoons sunflower oil

2 tablespoons chopped fresh ginger root

1 lemon grass stalk, bruised and coarsely chopped

1 green chile, halved, seeded, and chopped

1 red chile, halved, seeded, and chopped

1 large garlic clove, crushed

1 small bunch of cilantro, stems and leaves

3 scallions, coarsely chopped

Place all the curry paste ingredients and 2 tablespoons of the coconut milk in a small food processor and process together until smooth.

Heat a wok or large skillet, add the paste and cook over medium heat, stirring constantly, for 2 minutes.

Add the remaining coconut milk and stock and bring to a boil. Add the cauliflower florets to the broth, reduce the heat and simmer for 8–10 minutes, until just cooked.

Heat the oil for deep-frying in a deep-fat fryer or deep saucepan to 350–375°F, or until a cube of bread browns in 30 seconds. Add the noodles to the hot oil in small batches and fry for 30 seconds, until golden and crisp. Remove, draining off the excess oil, and transfer to paper towels to drain more.

Add the spinach to the broth and simmer for an additional 30 seconds. Stir in the cashew nuts.

To serve, ladle the Thai broth into 4 warmed serving bowls. Place some crisp-fried noodles on top of each and a sprinkling of cilantro leaves. Serve straight away.

*Soups are so simple and offer a speedy, tasty, and nutritious meal. I love to add a little sexiness, such as the Fresh Chili Relish used here. It's also fab as an accompaniment to curry or shellfish.*

# Spiced Sweet Potato Chowder

## SERVES 4

2 tablespoons store-bought curry paste, such as Madras or korma if you like it milder

1 onion, finely chopped

12oz potatoes, peeled and cut into ¾-inch cubes

1 large sweet potato, peeled and cut into ¾-inch cubes

¾ cup dried red split lentils, washed

3¾ cups vegetable stock

⅔ cup coconut cream, plus extra for drizzling

salt and pepper

### FRESH CHILI RELISH

½ bunch of scallions, finely chopped

1 red chile, seeded and finely chopped

1 small bunch of flat leaf parsley, leaves picked

squeeze of lime juice

2 teaspoons olive oil

Heat a saucepan, add the curry paste and cook over medium heat, stirring constantly, for 2 minutes. Stir in the onion, cover with a lid and steam-fry for 5 minutes, stirring occasionally.

Add the potatoes, sweet potato, lentils, and stock to the pan. Bring to a boil, then reduce the heat and simmer for 20 minutes or until the potatoes are just tender.

Meanwhile, for the fresh chili relish, simply toss all the ingredients together in a bowl and then spoon into a serving bowl. Set to one side.

Stir ⅔ cup of the coconut cream into the soup and season to taste with salt and pepper. Stir a little extra coconut cream in a small bowl until smooth.

Ladle the soup into warmed bowls. Using a spoon, drizzle in a little coconut cream and top with the Fresh Chili Relish. Serve with mango chutney and pappadams.

*I don't know why barley is such an underrated grain; maybe it's just because it sounds rather old-fashioned. But here it is the hero grain! It has a delicious nutty flavor and creates a lovely, creamy texture once cooked. Use in soups, stews, and risotto-like dishes. Any leftovers can be reheated risotto style and served with your favorite sausages or pork chops with a good dollop of mustard.*

# Barley Minestrone with Fava Bean & Basil Pistou

### SERVES 4

6 cups chicken or vegetable stock

½ cup dried pearl barley

2 tablespoons olive oil

1 leek, trimmed, cleaned, and finely chopped

2 celery sticks, finely chopped

2 large carrots, peeled and finely chopped

1 parsnip, peeled and finely chopped

2 bay leaves

1 tablespoon thyme leaves

2 tablespoons tomato paste

5 tablespoons white wine

2 tablespoons chopped parsley

salt and pepper

¼ cup Fava Bean & Basil Pistou or Classic Pesto (see page 184), to serve

Pour the stock into a large bowl, add the pearl barley and set aside for 30 minutes.

Heat the oil in a large saucepan, add the leek, celery, carrots, parsnip, bay, and thyme and cook over medium heat for 5 minutes.

Stir in the tomato paste and cook for 3 minutes. Pour in the wine and the stock and pearl barley and bring to a boil, then reduce the heat and simmer for 15–20 minutes.

Stir in the parsley and season to taste with salt and pepper. Pour into warmed bowls and serve with the pistou or pesto.

*It's fast, it's healthy, and best of all it's really tasty! Blitzing half the potatoes with the soy milk and stock really makes this chowder creamy without having to add any cream. Serve with warm Bacon & Sage Cornbread (see page 142) or Chive & Cheese Soda Bread (see page 142).*

# Creamy Corn & Haddock Chowder

## SERVES 4

1 tablespoon olive oil

1 onion, finely chopped

1lb potatoes, peeled and cut into ¾-inch cubes

2½ cups fish or vegetable stock

1¼ cups soy milk

1 cup canned corn kernels in water, drained

14½oz skinless undyed smoked haddock or cod fillets, cut into bite-size pieces

2 tablespoons chopped parsley

salt and pepper

Heat the oil in a large saucepan, add the onion and cook for 5 minutes. Add the potatoes and cook for another minute.

Pour in the stock, cover with a lid and simmer for 12–15 minutes or until the potatoes are tender. Using a slotted spoon, remove half the potatoes from the stock and set to one side.

Place the remaining potatoes, stock, and soy milk in a blender and carefully blitz until smooth. Pour back into the pan.

Add the corn kernels and simmer for 2 minutes. Stir in the smoked fish and reserved potatoes and cook for another 3–4 minutes. Stir in the parsley and season to taste with salt and pepper.

Ladle into 4 warmed bowls and serve straight away.

*Frozen peas are a must in the freezer so that you can whip up this creamy chowder whenever you want. Serve with garlic bread or try it with the super-speedy Skillet Scones (see below).*

# Pea & Bacon Chowder

### SERVES 4

1 tablespoon olive oil

1 onion, finely chopped

1 garlic clove, crushed

4½ cups frozen petits pois

3 cups vegetable stock

salt and pepper

TO SERVE

8 bacon slices

handful of arugula leaves

Heat the oil in a saucepan, add the onion and cook over medium heat for 5–6 minutes, until softened. Add the garlic and cook for another minute.

Stir in three-quarters of the petits pois and pour in the stock. Bring to a boil, then reduce the heat and simmer for 10–12 minutes. Transfer to a blender or food processor and blend until smooth.

Return the soup to the pan and add the remaining petits pois. Bring to a boil and then simmer for 2 minutes. Season to taste.

Meanwhile, preheat the broiler to high. Broil the bacon until crisp.

Ladle the soup into warmed bowls and top with bacon and arugula leaves.

# Skillet Scones

### SERVES 4

2½ cups all-purpose flour, plus extra for dusting

1½ tablespoons baking powder

3 tablespoons canola or olive oil

1 tablespoon almond milk (see page 177 for homemade)

1 egg, beaten

⅔ cup dairy-free light cream

2 tablespoons chopped parsley

salt and pepper

Sift the flour and baking powder into a large bowl. Season well.

Mix together half the oil, the almond milk, egg, and dairy-free cream in a large pitcher, then stir in the parsley. Pour the wet ingredients into the dry and gently combine to form a soft and manageable dough.

Gently roll out the dough on a lightly floured surface into a 6-inch circle about ¾ inch thick. Cut out into 8 wedges.

Place a large, nonstick skillet over medium heat and add the remaining oil. Add the scones to the pan and cook for about 8–10 minutes on each side until browned and cooked through. Serve warm.

# Weekday Favorites

*Simply take this dish of delicious, spicy everyday veggies topped
with eggs and wilted spinach to the table in the pan it's cooked
in and serve straight away. You will need a really good nonstick
skillet for this recipe.*

# Pan-fried Vegetable Bhaji with Eggs & Wilted Greens

### SERVES 4

¼ cup medium curry paste, such as Madras or rogan josh

1lb potatoes, peeled and shredded

2 leeks, trimmed, cleaned, and finely shredded

2 carrots, peeled and shredded

1 tablespoon coconut oil

4 free-range eggs

large handful of baby spinach leaves, finely shredded

salt and pepper

Heat a small saucepan, add the curry paste and cook over medium heat, stirring constantly, for 3 minutes to bring out the flavors.

With your hands, squeeze out as much liquid as possible from the shredded potatoes. Place them in a large bowl with the leeks and carrots. Stir in the curry paste, season well with salt and pepper and toss everything together until the veggies are thoroughly coated—to be honest, I normally use my hands for this.

Preheat the broiler to medium.

Spoon the coconut oil into a large, nonstick skillet, add the vegetables and make 4 indentations in the top of the bhaji. Cook over medium heat for 10 minutes, until golden underneath.

Place the pan under the broiler and cook for 8–10 minutes or until the bhaji is golden on top. Remove from the brioler.

Crack and pour an egg into each indentation and grind over a little black pepper. Place back over medium heat on the stove, cover with a lid and cook for about 5–6 minutes or until the eggs are cooked to your desire.

Sprinkle with the spinach and take to the table to serve.

*I promise you that once you've made hummus with lima beans instead of chickpeas, there is no going back. The nutty spice mix Dukkah is good to serve alongside—dip the bread first in the oil and then into the Dukkah.*

# White Bean Creamy Hummus with Fava Bean Salad & Dukkah

### SERVES 4

1 (14oz) can lima beans, drained and rinsed

¼ cup tahini paste

1 garlic clove, coarsely chopped

juice of 1 lemon

½ cup olive oil

2 tablespoons warm water

1 small bunch of flat leaf parsley, leaves picked

⅔ cup skinned cooked fava beans

2 tablespoons pine nuts, toasted

½ teaspoon dried red pepper flakes

### DUKKAH

2 tablespoons sesame seeds

1 tablespoon cumin seeds

½ tablespoon ground coriander

3 tablespoons whole blanched almonds, toasted

### TO SERVE

4 flatbreads, warmed

1 large bunch of radishes, trimmed

olive oil, for dipping

Place the lima beans, tahini paste, and garlic in a food processor and blend until smooth.

Add the lemon juice, 6 tablespoons of the oil, and the measured water, then blend again until very smooth. Season to taste with salt and pepper.

Mix together the parsley, fava beans, pine nuts, and red pepper flakes in a bowl. Set to one side.

For the Dukkah, toast the sesame seeds, cumin seeds, and ground coriander in a skillet pan for 2 minutes.

Place the almonds in a food processor with the toasted spices and season with salt and pepper. Pulse for just a few seconds until medium ground.

To serve, spread the hummus onto 4 serving plates. Sprinkle with the fava bean salad and drizzle each with the remaining oil. Serve with the warm flatbreads and crunchy radishes, together with the Dukkah for dipping.

Store the Dukkah in a sterilized Kilner or other preserving jar or jam jar in a cool, dark place—it will keep for up to 4 weeks in an airtight container. It makes a great crust for roasting salmon or chicken, or sprinkle it over your fave salad or homemade soups.

*The very simplest, tastiest pasta dish, this is also a real pantry savior. Crispy crumbs and pasta may sound a bit bonkers, but I promise you it really works.*

# Basil & Bean Linguine with Crispy Crumbs

### SERVES 4

12oz dried linguine

½ cup extra virgin olive oil

¼ cup focaccia or dairy-free fresh white bread crumbs

2 red chiles, seeded and finely chopped

2 garlic cloves, crushed

1 large bunch of basil leaves

2 x (14oz) cans cranberry beans, drained and rinsed

juice of 1 lemon

salt and pepper

Cook the pasta according to the package instructions.

Meanwhile, heat 2 tablespoons of the oil in a medium-size skillet pan, stir in the bread crumbs and cook over medium heat for about 5 minutes, until golden and crisp. Transfer to a small bowl.

Return the pan to medium heat, add the remaining oil, the chiles, garlic, and basil and cook for 30 seconds or until the basil turns bright green. Add the beans and heat through. Add the lemon juice and season well with salt and pepper.

To serve, drain the cooked pasta and toss through the hot basil beans. Pile into 4 warmed serving bowls and sprinkle with the crispy crumbs. Grind over some black pepper and serve at once.

*It doesn't get much easier than this! The size of the pan, however, is really important—it needs to have a wide base and be fairly shallow. For this dish you need good-quality, flavorsome ingredients. Good is simple; simple is good!*

# Altogether Pasta Pronto

### SERVES 4

3 tablespoons extra virgin olive oil

11oz dried tagliatelle

1lb large ripe plum tomatoes, coarsely chopped

1 bunch of scallions, coarsely chopped

3 large garlic cloves, crushed

1 teaspoon dried red pepper flakes

4 cups water

1 small bunch of basil leaves, torn

salt and pepper

Add 2 tablespoons of the oil to a large sauté pan, then arrange the tagliatelle nests in the pan in a single layer. Top with the tomatoes, scallions, garlic, and pepper flakes. Pour over the measured water and season really well with salt and pepper.

Place over high heat, cover with a lid and bring to a boil. Remove the lid once boiling and cook over high heat for 10–12 minutes, tossing the pasta regularly until it is al dente and the liquid has been almost all absorbed.

Stir through the basil leaves, season to taste with salt and pepper and drizzle over the remaining oil. Take in the pan to the table to serve.

*For the times when only something cheesy will do, treat yourself to this tasty cheat's version of the well-loved classic. I have fond memories of mum's sliced tomatoes on top of this family favorite, but I've brought it right up to date by using roasted chilied vine tomatoes and crispy bacon.*

# Double-baked Mac & Cheese with Roasted Vine Tomatoes

### SERVES 4

¼ cup olive oil

¼ cup all-purpose flour

1 tablespoon Dijon mustard

3¾ cups soy milk

1½ cups finely grated dairy-free sharp cheddar-style cheese

freshly grated nutmeg, to taste

10oz dried macaroni, cooked according to the package instructions

3 tablespoons dairy-free fresh white bread crumbs

13oz baby vine tomatoes, kept on the vine

chili or olive oil, for drizzling (optional)

6 rindless smoked bacon slices

salt and pepper

Preheat the oven to 400°F.

Heat 3 tablespoons of the oil in a large saucepan, add the flour and mustard and cook over medium heat for 30 seconds. Remove from the heat and add all the soy milk. Beat well until all the lumps have gone, then return to heat and bring to a boil, stirring constantly. Simmer for 4–5 minutes, until thickish and smooth.

Add three-quarters of the dairy-free cheese, remove from the heat and stir until melted. Season to taste with nutmeg and salt and pepper.

Stir the cooked macaroni into the sauce and transfer to a large or 2 medium-size, shallow ovenproof dishes. Mix together the remaining cheese and the bread crumbs and sprinkle over the dish.

Bake for about 15 minutes, until golden and bubbling hot and a good crust has formed.

Remove the mac and cheese from the oven, lay the tomato vine over the top and drizzle with chili or olive oil, if using, then return to the oven for another 8–10 minutes.

Meanwhile, broil or fry the bacon until crisp.

Crumble the bacon over the mac and cheese and serve at once.

*The pea puree flavored with sweet basil is the special element in this dish. Not only does it taste divine and have a wonderful vibrant color, but it makes the risotto super rich and velvety.*

# Summer Fresh Pea & Dried Tomato Risotto

**SERVES 4 AS AN APPETIZER
OR 2 AS A MAIN COURSE**

### PEA PUREE

2 tablespoons olive oil

1 onion, finely chopped

1 cup frozen petits pois

¾ cup boiling water

1 cup basil, stems and leaves

salt and pepper

### RISOTTO

20 semidried tomatoes in oil, drained and 2 tablespoons of the oil reserved

1 onion, finely chopped

2 garlic cloves, crushed

¾ cup risotto rice

⅔ cup white wine

1 tablespoon olive oil

3 cups hot vegetable stock

1 cup podded fresh peas

To make the pea puree, heat the olive oil in a medium-size, shallow skillet, add the onion and cook over medium heat for 5 minutes or until softened.

Add the petits pois and the measured water and season well with salt and pepper. Bring to a boil, cover with a lid and cook for 2 minutes. Stir in all the basil and cook for 1 minute.

Transfer the pea mixture to a blender and puree until smooth. Season to taste with salt and pepper and set to one side to cool.

To make the risotto, heat the tomato oil in a saucepan. Stir in the onion and cook for 5 minutes or until softened. Add the garlic and cook for another 2 minutes.

Stir in the rice and cook for 1 minute. Pour in the white wine, add the oil and cook until absorbed.

Add half the hot stock, a ladleful at a time, stirring until each addition is almost all absorbed into the rice—this will take approximately 10 minutes. Add the peas and continue adding the remaining stock as before, until the rice is cooked but still al dente —this will take approximately 8–10 minutes. Season to taste with salt and pepper.

To serve, mix the pea puree into the risotto, spoon into warmed serving dishes and top with the tomatoes.

*Cremini mushrooms are the brown form of the common mushroom, and I think they always taste and look more interesting than the white sort. Large field mushrooms have a good woodland flavor that works wonderfully well with the dry sherry. Serve it on sourdough toasts with the crunchy walnut and arugula salad for real posh mushrooms on toast.*

# Mushroom Stroganoff with Walnuts & Arugula

### SERVES 4

2 tablespoons olive oil

1 large garlic clove, crushed

1lb cremini mushrooms, thickly sliced

12oz flat field mushrooms, peeled and thickly sliced

1 tablespoon all-purpose flour

⅔ cup dry sherry

¾ cup vegetable stock, plus extra if needed

1 bunch of thyme, coarsely chopped

⅔ cup dairy-free light cream

1¾ cups arugula leaves

¾ cup walnut halves, toasted and crumbled

drizzle of extra virgin olive oil

1 tablespoon good-quality balsamic vinegar

4 thick slices of dairy-free rustic or sourdough bread, toasted

salt and pepper

Heat the olive oil in a large frying pan or sauté pan, add the garlic and cook over medium heat for 30 seconds. Add the mushrooms and cook over high heat for 4–5 minutes or until colored.

Sprinkle with the flour and cook for 1 minute. Stir in the sherry, stock, and the thyme, season well with salt and pepper and simmer for 10–15 minutes.

Add the cream to the mushrooms and simmer for another 5 minutes, adding extra stock if the stroganoff looks too thick —it should be the consistency of a thick gravy.

Toss the arugula leaves and walnuts with the extra virgin olive oil and balsamic vinegar in a bowl.

To serve, top the toasted sourdough with the stroganoff and serve with the arugula and walnut salad.

*These delicious toasted melts will really hit the spot! This is one of my favorite flavor combinations: creamy cider and cheese topped with air-cured ham.*

# Welsh Rarebit Melts

### SERVES 4

1 cup finely grated dairy-free cheddar-style cheese

1 tablespoon English mustard

2 tablespoons hard cider or white wine

5 tablespoons dairy-free light cream

8 large slices of dairy-free sourdough bread, about ¾ inch thick

1 red onion, finely sliced

3 tablespoons olive oil, plus extra if needed

4 slices of air-cured ham

1¾ cups arugula leaves

Preheat the oven to 400°F.

Mix together the cheese, mustard, cider or white wine, and cream in a bowl. Spread over 4 of the bread slices, sprinkle with the red onion and sandwich together with the remaining bread slices. Cut each in half so that you end up with 8 melts.

Heat half the oil in a large, nonstick skillet over a medium heat. Add 2 of the melts and cook for about 1–2 minutes on each side until golden. Transfer to a baking sheet. Repeat with the remaining melts, adding the remaining oil. Place the melts in the oven for about 4–5 minutes, until oozy in the middle.

Meanwhile, place the air-cured ham in the pan, adding the remaining oil if necessary, and fry over medium heat until crispy.

Toss the arugula with a little olive oil in a bowl.

To serve, place 2 melts on each serving plate and top with the crispy ham, with a side of lightly dressed arugula leaves.

*Here's a variation on paella using small pasta instead of rice,*
*which gives a lighter result. Simply take to the table in its pan and*
*serve family style with a pile of Garlic Toasts.*

# Pasta Paella with Basil Ink

## SERVES 4–6

6 tablespoons olive oil

1 large onion, chopped

1 tablespoon smoked paprika

10oz small dried pasta
—I used chifferi rigati—
or you could use macaroni

5 cups vegetable stock

1½ cups frozen baby fava beans

1 cup cherry tomatoes, halved

1 large garlic clove, crushed

1 small bunch of basil

1 tablespoon cold water

1 (7oz) can albacore tuna steak in olive oil (or any other good-quality canned tuna), lightly drained

2 tablespoons baby capers, drained

salt and pepper

### GARLIC TOASTS

4 thick-cut slices of dairy-free country-style bread

1 large garlic clove, peeled but kept whole

2 tablespoons extra virgin olive oil

2 tablespoons chopped parsley

pepper

Heat 2 tablespoons of the oil in a large, shallow sauté pan, add the onion and gently fry until softened and lightly colored. Stir in the paprika and cook for another 2 minutes.

Add the pasta and half the stock, then season well with salt and pepper, cover with a lid and simmer for 10 minutes.

Remove the lid from the pan and stir in the fava beans, tomatoes, and remaining stock. Bring to a boil, then replace the lid, reduce the heat and simmer for another 5–6 minutes.

Meanwhile, for the garlic toasts, preheat the broiler to medium. Toast the bread on both sides. Remove the toast from the broiler and, while hot, rub with the garlic clove. Drizzle over the oil, sprinkle with the parsley and season with pepper. Pile onto a serving board and set to one side.

To make the basil ink, place the remaining oil, garlic, basil, and measured water in a small blender and blend until smooth. Season to taste with salt and pepper.

Arrange the tuna and capers over the pasta but do not stir. Drizzle over the basil ink, grind over a little black pepper and take to the table in its pan. Serve with the Garlic Toasts.

*Fish pie in a flash! These light and delicate pies are so simple to put together, with the fish steaming in the stock, wine, and cream. Use fresh, ready-made phyllo pastry and then any leftovers can be frozen for later use. Serve with Creamy Garlic Mash (opposite).*

# Fish Cachets

### SERVES 4

2 tablespoons olive oil, plus extra for brushing

1 leek, trimmed, halved, cleaned, and cut into thin strips

2 large carrots, peeled and cut into thin strips

7oz skinless salmon fillet, cut into 1¼-inch chunks

10oz white fish fillets, such as lemon sole, pollock, cod, or haddock, skinned, any stray bones removed, and cut into 1¼-inch chunks

3½oz cooked peeled shrimp

⅔ cup fish stock

2 tablespoons white wine

¼ cup dairy-free light cream

4 sheets of fresh phyllo pastry

salt and pepper

Preheat the oven to 400°F.

Heat the oil in a skillet and stir in the vegetables. Cook over gentle heat for 4 minutes, until softened but not colored. Season to taste with salt and pepper and spoon equally among 4 small, ovenproof soup bowls. Set to one side to cool.

Divide the fish evenly on top of the vegetables and top with the shrimp. Drizzle over the stock, wine, and cream, and season well with salt and pepper.

Unroll the pastry and brush one sheet with oil. Cut in half, then slightly scrunch one half and lay over the top of the soup bowl, allowing it to drape over slightly. Scrunch the remaining half and place on top. Repeat with the remaining 3 soup bowls.

Place the bowls on a baking sheet and bake for about 20–25 minutes, until the pastry is golden and crisp and the fish and sauce are bubbling hot. Serve straight away.

*Roasting the garlic gives it a much softer, sweeter flavor and its richness gives the mash an almost buttery taste. See below for other flavor additions.*

# Creamy Garlic Mash

### SERVES 4

2 whole garlic bulbs

1¾lb floury potatoes, such as russet or Yukon gold

about ⅔ cup dairy-free milk

2 tablespoons olive oil

salt and pepper

Preheat the oven to 400°F.

Wrap the garlic bulbs in foil, place on a baking sheet and roast for 30 minutes.

Meanwhile, peel the potatoes and cut into even 2-inch pieces. Place in a medium-size saucepan, cover with cold water and add a pinch of salt.

Bring the potatoes to a boil, then reduce the heat and simmer for about 15–20 minutes or until tender. Drain the potatoes and immediately return to the saucepan. Mash over the heat for 30 seconds to evaporate any excess water.

Place the milk in a small saucepan and heat. Remove the garlic from the oven and, when cool enough to handle, carefully squeeze the pulp from the garlic cloves into the milk along with the olive oil. Mash together until smooth and stir through the mash. Season to taste with salt and pepper and serve. Alternatively, for a completely smooth mash, push the potatoes through a potato ricer, then stir in the garlic milk.

*Creamy Mustard Mash*
Omit the garlic and add 2 tablespoons whole-grain mustard, or to taste, and 3 tablespoons chopped parsley with the milk.

*Creamy Horseradish Mash*
Omit the garlic and add 3–4 tablespoons dairy-free creamed horseradish sauce with the milk. Top your mash with freshly chopped chives.

*Creamy and rich with a touch of freshness with lemon and chives, this is a kind of deconstructed fish pie without all the fuss and using only one pan and one serving dish. It makes a great family weekday supper dish. These potatoes are also good served straight from the pan with baked ham or roast chicken.*

# Creamy Lemon Potatoes
# with Herby Salmon

## SERVES 4

1¼ cups almond milk (see page 177 for homemade) or other dairy-free milk

1 cup dairy-free light cream

grated zest of 1 unwaxed lemon and juice of ½

1 garlic clove, crushed

1¾lb potatoes, peeled and cut into about ¾-inch cubes

4 skinless salmon fillets, about 4½oz each

1 tablespoon olive oil

1 small bunch of chives, chopped

1½ cups frozen petits pois

salt and pepper

Preheat the oven to 400°F.

Place the milk, cream, lemon zest, and garlic in a nonstick sauté pan and season generously with salt and pepper. Heat gently until just boiling.

Add the potatoes to the pan and bring back to a boil. Reduce the heat and simmer over medium heat for about 20 minutes or until the potatoes are just tender and still holding their shape.

Meanwhile, place the salmon fillets in a bowl, drizzle over the lemon juice and oil and sprinkle with the chives, then season well with salt and pepper. Mix well to coat the salmon fillets.

Add the peas to the potatoes and gently stir through, then pour into a gratin dish. Lay the salmon fillets over the top and bake for 15 minutes, until cooked through. Serve with a watercress salad.

# Fiery Fish Pie

### SERVES 4–6

2½lb potatoes, peeled and cut into even-size chunks

1¼lb skinless salmon fillet, cut into 31¼–1¾-inch chunks

12oz skinless cod fillet

1¾ cups fish stock

⅓ cup white wine

3 tablespoons dairy-free spread

1 small onion, finely chopped

2–3 hot red chilies, seeded and finely chopped

⅓ cup all-purpose flour

1 cup dairy-free light cream

8oz cooked peeled jumbo shrimp

1 tablespoon olive oil

2 teaspoons ground turmeric

⅓ cup dairy-free milk, warmed

salt and pepper

Preheat the oven to 425°F.

Place the potatoes in a large saucepan of cold water and bring to a boil, then reduce the heat and simmer for 20 minutes or until tender.

Meanwhile, place the salmon and cod in a large, shallow saucepan. Pour over the stock and white wine and bring to a boil, then reduce the heat, cover with a lid and simmer for 5 minutes. Remove the fish and transfer to a 2-quart ovenproof or gratin dish. Strain the cooking liquid and set to one side.

Melt the spread in a saucepan. Add the onion and chilies and cook gently for 5 minutes or until softened but not colored. Stir in the flour and cook for 1 minute. Gradually beat in the reserved cooking liquid and simmer for 5 minutes.

Stir in the cream and shrimp and cook for 2 minutes. Season to taste with salt and pepper and pour over the fish.

Drain the potatoes well. Put back into the pan over low heat, then mash, adding the oil, turmeric, and milk. Season to taste with salt and pepper.

Spoon the mash over the fish and mark the surface with a fork. Bake for 25–30 minutes until golden and bubbling hot. Serve with snow peas, green beans, or broccoli.

*Rich, oily fish like mackerel works really well with Indian-style spices. To release the flavor from your coriander seeds, place in a plastic bag and bash with a rolling pin—it's worth the extra effort.*

# Cracked Coriander Grilled Mackerel Fillets with Spiced Orange Lentils

### SERVES 4

2 tablespoons coriander seeds, crushed

1 tablespoon coarsely ground black pepper

¼ cup coarsely chopped flat leaf parsley

8 small mackerel fillets

1 tablespoon olive oil

### LENTILS

1 tablespoon sunflower oil

1 large onion, chopped

4 garlic cloves, crushed

1 tablespoon garam masala

11¾ cups dried orange lentils, washed

5 cups vegetable stock

4 cups spinach leaves, coarsely chopped

### RELISH

1 large red onion, finely chopped

2 large ripe tomatoes, finely chopped

1 tablespoon chopped mint leaves

squeeze of lemon juice

salt and pepper

Mix together the crushed coriander, black pepper, and parsley in a bowl. Rub the flesh side of the mackerel fillets with the olive oil, press over the spice mix and set to one side.

For the lentils, heat the sunflower oil in a large skillet, add the onion and gently fry for 5 minutes. Add the garlic and garam masala and cook for another minute. Add the lentils and stock to the pan and bring to a boil, then reduce the heat and simmer for 15–20 minutes or until the lentils are just tender.

To make the relish, simply mix all the ingredients together and season to taste with salt and pepper. Set to one side.

Heat a ridged grill pan, add the mackerel skin side down and cook over medium-high heat for 2–3 minutes, then turn over and cook for 1–2 minutes on the other side, until just cooked through.

To serve, stir the spinach into the lentils and spoon onto 4 warmed serving plates. Top each serving with 2 mackerel fillets and serve at once with the relish.

*Don't be put off by the amount of garlic used here: because it is baked in its skin, it becomes deliciously sweet. Chicken thighs are juicy and full of flavor, but it's best to use skinless ones, as it keeps the sauce grease free.*

# Garlic & Thyme Chicken with Cannellini & Potato Mash

### SERVES 4

¼ cup olive or canola oil

8 large skinless chicken thighs

⅔ cup chicken stock

1 cup red wine

1 whole garlic bulb, separated into cloves but kept unpeeled

1 small bunch of thyme, broken into sprigs

1 large bay leaf

1 orange, halved

1¾lb floury white potatoes, such as russet or Yukon gold, peeled and cut into even-size chunks

1 (15oz) can cannellini beans, drained and rinsed

¼ cup dairy-free milk

2 tablespoons chopped flat leaf parsley

¼ cup balsamic vinegar

pinch of sugar

salt and pepper

Preheat the oven to 375°F.

Place a medium-size, heavy roasting pan on the stove over medium heat, add half the oil and lay in the chicken thighs. Season with a little salt and lots of pepper. Fry the chicken thighs for a few minutes until beginning to colour. Meanwhile, mix together the stock and red wine in a pitcher.

Add the garlic cloves, thyme sprigs, and the bay leaf to the roasting pan. Squeeze over the juice from the orange halves and add in the squeezed halves. Pour in one-third of the wine and stock mixture and toss together well.

Bake the chicken pieces for about 30 minutes, turning over halfway through cooking, until cooked through—the juices should run clear when pierced through the thickest part with the tip of a knife.

Meanwhile, cook the potatoes in a saucepan of boiling water for 20–25 minutes, until tender. Drain and return to the pan. Add the cannellini beans, milk, and remaining oil and mash together. Stir in the parsley and season well with salt and pepper. Keep warm.

Place the chicken thighs in a serving dish along with half the garlic cloves, the orange halves, and bay. Set to one side and keep warm. Squeeze the pulp from the remaining garlic cloves into the roasting pan. Place the pan on the stove over medium heat, add the balsamic vinegar, remaining wine and stock mixture, and the sugar and bring to a boil. Use a wooden spoon to scrape up the sediment from the bottom of the pan and mash in the garlic pulp. Simmer over high heat for about 4 minutes or until syrupy. Season to taste with salt and pepper.

Pour the sauce over the chicken and serve with the cannellini and potato mash, along with lightly dressed baby spinach leaves.

*This is a modern, speedy version of a classic French dish. The chorizo crumbs really give the chicken some oomph—you could use salami or blood sausage in the crumb mixture instead. The creamy apple cassoulet is also great served with sausages or pork chops, or as a side dish with roast chicken.*

# Chorizo-crusted Chicken with Apple & Sage Cassoulet

### SERVES 4

4 small boneless, skinless chicken breasts

4oz sliced cured chorizo sausage, very coarsely chopped

4½ cups dairy-free coarse fresh white bread crumbs

2 free-range eggs, beaten

about 5 tablespoons olive or canola oil

### CASSOULET

3 dessert apples, quartered, cored, and coarsely chopped

2 red onions, finely chopped

1 (15oz) can cannellini beans, drained and rinsed

¾ cup hard cider

¾ cup chicken stock

2 teaspoons Dijon mustard

¾ cup dairy-free light cream

1 tablespoon chopped sage

1 tablespoon chopped parsley

salt and pepper

Preheat the oven to 325°F.

Place a chicken breast between 2 sheets of plastic wrap and gently bat out with a rolling pin until almost doubled in size. Repeat with the remaining chicken breasts.

Place the chorizo in a food processor and pulse until finely chopped. Add the bread crumbs and pulse until well mixed. Tip out onto a large plate.

Dip the chicken breasts in the beaten egg in a bowl and then coat with the chorizo crumbs.

Heat 2 tablespoons of the oil in a large, nonstick skillet, add 2 chicken breasts and cook for about 3–4 minutes on each side or until golden and completely cooked through. Remove from the pan and keep warm in the oven. Repeat with the remaining chicken breasts.

To make the cassoulet, return the pan to the heat, add the remaining oil, the apples, and the onions and cook over medium heat for 5 minutes.

Add the beans, cider, and stock and bring to a boil. Reduce the heat and simmer briskly until reduced by half.

Stir in the mustard, dairy-free cream, and herbs, and season to taste with salt and pepper.

Spoon the cassoulet into 4 warmed serving dishes. Cut each chicken breast into 3 thick slices and place on top. Serve straight away.

*A tortilla with a twist—tortillas sandwiched together
with a bean, chicken, and cheese filling, and cooked until
melting in the middle and golden on the outside.*

# Smoky Quesadilla Melts with Chicken, Cilantro & Avocado

<u>SERVES 4</u>

8 flour tortillas

1 (15oz) can mixed beans, drained, rinsed, and patted dry

1 bunch of scallions, finely chopped

5 tablespoons good-quality store-bought mayonnaise or Smoked Garlic & Chive Mayo (see page 185)

1 tablespoon whole-grain mustard

8oz cooked chicken breast, skinned and thinly sliced

1 (9½oz) jar chargrilled peppers in oil, drained and cut into chunky slices (or you could use the Sweet Pepper Chutney on page 181)

1 bunch of cilantro leaves, coarsely chopped

1 large mild red chile, finely chopped

1 large ripe avocado, halved, pitted, peeled, and sliced

1 cup finely grated smoked cheddar-style soy cheese, finely grated

¼ cup olive oil

1 lime, cut into wedges

pepper

Place 4 of the tortillas on a work surface.

Gently mix together the beans, scallions, mayonnaise, and mustard in a bowl. Season well with pepper and spread the mixture evenly over the tortillas.

Arrange the chicken and peppers over the top and sprinkle with the cilantro and chilli. Top with the avocado slices and finally sprinkle over the cheese.

Top each with one of the remaining flour tortillas and press down well to sandwich together.

Heat a medium-size, nonstick skillet and add 1 tablespoon of the oil. Using a large spatula, carefully lift and place a filled tortilla in the hot pan. Place a medium-size plate on the top and gently push down.

Cook over medium heat for about 4–5 minutes, then remove the plate and quickly and carefully turn the quesadilla over—don't worry if a little filling comes out; just push it back in! Cook for another 3–4 minutes, until dark golden and heated through. Remove from the pan and keep warm in a low oven while you repeat with the remaining quesadillas, using the remaining oil.

Cut each quesadilla into 4 wedges and pile on a serving board. Serve with the lime wedges.

*Succulent sesame chicken with a creamy hummus sauce—a marriage made in heaven! This fast marinade is also great with turkey and pork. Store-bought hummus works well when time is short, but if you fancy it, try using the homemade variety on page 60.*

# Sesame Chicken Lickin'

## SERVES 4

3 large boneless, skinless chicken breasts, about 6oz each, cut into finger strips

juice of 1 lemon

2 tablespoons olive oil

2 tablespoons whole-grain mustard

1 garlic clove, crushed

2 tablespoons honey

3 tablespoons sesame seeds

½ cucumber, peeled, seeded, and cut into small chunks

1 romaine lettuce, torn into bite-size pieces

2 large carrots, peeled and then peeled into ribbons with a vegetable peeler

salt and pepper

### SAUCE

¾ cup store-bought hummus

3 tablespoons dairy-free plain yogurt

squeeze of lemon juice, to taste

pepper

4 pita breads, to serve

Toss the chicken with the lemon juice, 1 tablespoon of the oil, the mustard, garlic, and honey in a bowl. Season well with salt and pepper. Cover the bowl with plastic wrap and set to one side for 10 minutes.

Heat the remaining oil in a large, nonstick wok or skillet until hot. Add the chicken to the pan, reserving the marinade, and stir-fry for 4 minutes. Sprinkle with the sesame seeds and cook for another 3–4 minutes, until the seeds are golden and the chicken is just cooked through.

Pour in the marinade, bring to a boil and swirl the pan well until the chicken is sticky.

Meanwhile, mix together the hummus and yogurt in a bowl. Season to taste with lemon juice and pepper.

To serve, toast the pita breads. Meanwhile, toss the salad ingredients together in a bowl. Divide the salad among 4 serving bowls and top each with the hot sesame chicken. Top with a dollop of the hummus sauce and serve with the toasted pitas.

*This is a lovely curry and a perfect family choice, as it's creamy and very mildly spiced. It can be served with rice, but I usually serve it with this Tomato & Chili Relish to cut through the richness. Homemade Socca bread (see page 139) and chapatis or crispy pappadams are also good accompaniments.*

# Creamy Chicken Curry

### SERVES 4

1 tablespoon coconut oil

1 onion, finely sliced

1 large garlic clove, crushed

1 tablespoon ground turmeric

2 teaspoons ground coriander

1 teaspoon ground cumin

1 small cinnamon stick

2 bay leaves

3 tablespoons unsweetened shredded coconut

3 large boneless, skinless chicken breasts, about 6oz each, cut into 2-inch chunks

1¾ cups chicken stock

1 cup coconut cream

2 cups spinach leaves, shredded

salt and pepper

TOMATO & CHILI RELISH

7oz baby plum tomatoes, quartered

2 red chilies, seeded and finely chopped

pinch of sugar

1 tablespoon canola oil

squeeze of lemon juice

Heat the coconut oil in a nonstick saucepan, add the onion and cook gently for 10 minutes, until softened. Stir in the garlic and cook for another minute.

Add the spices and bay leaves and cook for 1 minute.

Stir in the coconut and cook for 1 minute until toasted.

Add the chicken, toss in the spice mix and cook for 1 minute.

Pour in the stock and coconut cream and bring to a boil, then reduce the heat and simmer gently for 20 minutes.

To make the relish, simply mix all the ingredients together in a bowl, season to taste with salt and pepper and spoon into a serving dish.

Add the spinach to the curry and cook for 1 minute. Season to taste with salt and pepper.

Serve the curry with the relish.

*The new additions of fresh spinach and nutmeg really give this rich favorite a lighter, contemporary taste. If you fancy a fishy version simply toss through smoked salmon strips with the spinach at the end, leaving out the pancetta.*

# Spaghetti alla Carbonara

### SERVES 4

12oz dried spaghetti

2 tablespoons olive oil

4oz diced pancetta

2 large garlic cloves, crushed

3 large free-range eggs

¾ cup finely grated dairy-free cheddar-style cheese

1 cup spinach, finely shredded

freshly grated nutmeg, to taste

salt and pepper

Place a large saucepan of water on to boil and stir in a good pinch of salt. Add the spaghetti and cook for about 10 minutes or until al dente.

Meanwhile, heat the oil in a large skillet, add the pancetta and fry for 4–5 minutes until golden and crisp. Remove from the heat and stir in the garlic.

Beat the eggs together with the cheese in a bowl and season well with salt and pepper.

Drain the pasta, reserving some of the cooking liquid. Tip the pasta into the skillet with the pancetta and garlic, then add 2 tablespoons of the reserved cooking liquid.

Place the pan over medium heat and pour in the egg mixture. Using 2 wooden spoons, toss the spaghetti so that it mixes with the egg mixture and all the spaghetti is coated. Heat through until thickened, taking care not to overcook it or you will end up with scrambled egg!

At the last moment, stir through the spinach and season with plenty of black pepper and nutmeg. Serve straight away.

*I'm very fussy about my pizza—making your own pizza bases really is worth the effort, and this dough is easy to prepare. I have suggested some more pizza toppings below, but feel free to experiment. Enjoy!*

# Pizza Pizza Pizza

### MAKES 3 LARGE PIZZAS
### (EACH PIZZA SERVES 2)

1¼lb cherry tomatoes, quartered

2 garlic cloves, crushed

¼ cup tomato paste

3 tablespoons olive oil

### DOUGH

5 cups bread flour, plus extra for dusting

1 teaspoon salt

2 (¼oz) envelopes active dry yeast

about 1¼ cups warm water

4 tablespoons olive oil, plus extra for oiling

### CLASSIC TOPPING

(Makes enough for 1 pizza)

4–5 tablespoons Classic Pesto (see page 184)

⅔ cups arugula leaves

2oz thinly sliced salami, torn into strips

extra virgin olive oil, for drizzling

pepper

To make the pizza dough, sift the flour into a large bowl and then stir in the salt and yeast. Make a well in the center of the flour mixture and pour in the measured water and oil. Using a flat-bladed knife, draw the mixture in from the sides to form a soft, wet dough.

Knead the dough on a lightly floured surface for 10 minutes until smooth and elastic. Place the dough in a lightly oiled large bowl, cover with plastic wrap and let rise in a warm place for about 1 hour or until doubled in size.

Preheat the oven to 425°F. Place the risen dough on a lightly floured surface and knock back with a firm kneading. Divide the dough into 3 and roll each piece on a floured surface into a circle measuring about 12 inches. Place on lightly floured baking sheets or pizza stones.

Toss the tomato quarters with the garlic and tomato paste in a bowl and season well with salt and pepper. Divide the tomato mixture among the 3 pizza bases, pressing it down gently. Bake for about 20 minutes or until the pizza is crisp and the tomatoes have slightly caramelized.

To serve, finish each pizza with your chosen toppings, drizzle over a little olive oil and season with pepper.

*Italiano Topping*

Top with 6oz drained antipasti roasted peppers in oil, ½ cup pitted olives, and a handful of basil leaves. Finish with olive oil.

*Tropical Topping*

Sprinkle over ¼ diced pineapple and ¼ cup drained canned corn kernels, then crumble over 4 crisply broiled bacon slices.

*Any excuse for a quiche! I love to top mine with arugula leaves. My other favorite fillers are roasted peppers and pine nuts with my Classic Pesto (see page 184) spread on the base of the pastry shell.*

# Classic Quiche

## SERVES 6

PASTRY

2¼ cups all-purpose flour, plus extra for dusting

pinch of salt

½ cup dairy-free spread

1 egg, beaten

2–3 tablespoons cold water

FILLING

3 tablespoons whole-grain mustard

3½oz antipasti tomatoes in oil, drained and chopped

7oz smoked ham, cut into strips

1 cup finely grated dairy-free cheddar-style cheese

2 free-range eggs

2 free-range egg yolks

1 cup dairy-free light cream

1 cup oat or soy milk

1 small bunch of chives, chopped

SALAD TOPPING

1 tablespoon extra virgin olive oil

1 tablespoon balsamic vinegar

1 cup arugula leaves

Preheat the oven to 375°F.

Sift the flour into a bowl and stir in the salt. Add the spread in small pieces and lightly blend in with your fingertips until the mixture resembles fine bread crumbs. Alternatively, place the ingredients in a food processor and blend together. Gently mix in the egg and enough of the water to bind the pastry dough together. Pat into a rough, flat disk, wrap in plastic wrap and chill in the refrigerator for 30 minutes.

Roll out the pastry gently on a lightly floured surface and use to line an 11-inch loose-bottomed removeable tart pan. Cover with plastic wrap and chill in the refrigerator for 15 minutes.

Line the pastry shell with parchment paper, and half-fill with pie weights. Bake blind for 10 minutes. Remove the pastry shell from the oven and lift out the paper and weights. Return to the oven for another 5 minutes. Remove from oven and increase the temperature to 400°F.

For the filling, spoon the mustard over the base of the pastry shell, then top with the tomatoes, ham, and half the cheese. Beat together the eggs, egg yolks, cream, and milk in a bowl. Season well with salt and pepper and stir in the chives. Pour the mixture carefully into the pastry shell and sprinkle with the remaining cheese.

Bake for 25–30 minutes, until the filling is golden and just set.

Remove the quiche from the oven and let cool for 10 minutes, then transfer to a serving plate.

Mix together the olive oil and balsamic vinegar in a large bowl. Season to taste with salt and pepper. Toss in the arugula leaves and pile in the center of the quiche just before serving.

*This dish is often spoiled by soggy veg, but by roasting the cauliflower and broccoli, you not only intensify the flavor but get firmer florets! It's most important to rinse the veggies well, as the water clinging to them will help in the cooking.*

# Roasted Cauliflower & Broccoli Mornay with a Chorizo Crumb

### SERVES 4

¼ cup olive oil

1 cauliflower, broken into small–medium-size florets

8oz broccoli, broken into medium–large florets

¼ cup all-purpose flour

2½ cups soy milk

¾ cup finely grated dairy-free strong cheddar-style cheese

2 tablespoons dairy-free light cream

squeeze of lemon juice

4oz sliced cured chorizo sausage, coarsely chopped

1 cup dairy-free fresh white bread crumbs

salt and pepper

Preheat the oven to 400°F.

Spoon half the oil into a shallow, flameproof, ovenproof dish and place over medium heat.

Meanwhile, rinse the vegetable florets under cold water. Add the wet florets to the hot pan. Toss together and season well with salt and pepper. Rinse a circle of wax paper the size of the pan under cold water and place over the vegetables. Cover with a tight-fitting lid or foil, place in the oven and bake for about 18–20 minutes or until the veg are just tender.

While the veg are baking, heat the remaining oil in a saucepan, add the flour and cook over medium heat for 30 seconds. Remove from the heat and add all the soy milk. Beat well until all the lumps have gone, then return to the heat and bring to a boil, stirring constantly. Simmer for 4–5 minutes, until thickish and smooth. Add the dairy-free cheese and cream, remove from the heat and stir until melted. Stir in the lemon juice and season to taste with salt and pepper.

For the crumbs, add the chorizo to a food processor and process until finely chopped. Place a medium-size skillet over a medium heat, add the chopped chorizo and fry for 3–4 minutes, until golden. Add the bread crumbs to the pan and fry for 2–3 minutes. Set to one side.

Remove the vegetable florets from the oven, pour over the mornay sauce and sprinkle with the chorizo crumbs. Return to the oven for 12–15 minutes, until bubbling and golden. Serve at once.

*Homemade lasagna without too much faff! This classic favorite is enhanced with red wine, large white mushrooms, and a thin layer of prosciutto ham, all topped off with a thick layer of no-cook creamy cheese sauce. Make sure you choose dried lasagna sheets that need no precooking, which are widely available and mostly dairy free.*

# Luxury Beef & Prosciutto Lasagna with a Cheesy Nutmeg Sauce

### SERVES 6

2 tablespoons olive oil

1 large onion, chopped

2 garlic cloves, crushed

8oz large white mushrooms, peeled and chopped

13oz good-quality lean ground beef

⅔ cup red wine

2 cups tomato puree or tomato sauce

1 (14½oz) can diced tomatoes

1 tablespoon thyme leaves

2 bay leaves

1 cup dairy-free cream cheese

⅔ cup dairy-free light cream

¾ cup finely grated dairy-free sharp cheddar-style cheese

good grating of nutmeg

6 no-precook sheets of dried lasagna

4 slices of prosciutto ham

salt and pepper

Preheat the oven to 400°F.

Heat the oil in a large, nonstick saucepan until hot. Stir in the onion and cook over medium heat for 4–5 minutes or until softened. Stir in the garlic, add the mushrooms and cook over high heat until all the liquid has evaporated.

Stir in the ground beef and fry, breaking up with a wooden spoon, for 4–5 minutes, until browned. Add the red wine, tomato puree or sauce, canned tomatoes, and herbs and season well with salt and pepper. Simmer for 25–30 minutes.

Meanwhile, for the cheese sauce, stir together the cream cheese, cream, and two-thirds of the grated cheese and season with the nutmeg and salt and pepper.

Spoon half the meat sauce into a nonstick roasting pan or shallow ovenproof dish about 8 inches x 10 inches. Top with 3 lasagna sheets and then with the remaining meat sauce and another 3 lasagna sheets. Lay over the prosciutto ham, pour over the cheese sauce and sprinkle with the remaining grated cheese.

Bake for about 30–35 minutes, until bubbling and golden.

*The muscovado and vinegar in these thick, tomato-coated beans create a wonderful sweet and sour flavour. The dumplings are quick to whip up and make a tasty and lighter alternative to the classic suet dumpling.*

# Boston Bean Bake Topped with Olive Oil & Herb Dumplings

### SERVES 4

1 tablespoon olive oil, plus extra for drizzling

1 large onion, chopped

1 large garlic clove, crushed

1 (14 oz) can borlotti beans, drained and rinsed

1 (15oz) can navy beans, drained and rinsed

1 tablespoon Dijon mustard

2 tablespoons packed light brown sugar

2 tablespoons white wine vinegar

2 cups tomato puree or tomato sauce

⅔ cup water

12 chipolata sausages

DUMPLINGS

1¾ cups all-purpose flour

1¾ teaspoons baking powder

3 tablespoons chopped parsley

1 tablespoon chopped sage

1 tablespoon thyme leaves

2 tablespoons olive oil

⅔ cup oat or other dairy-free milk

salt and pepper

Preheat the oven to 400°F.

Heat the oil in a flameproof casserole dish or other ovenproof pan, add the onion and cook for 5–6 minutes, until golden and softened. Add the garlic and cook for 1 minute.

Stir in the beans, mustard, sugar, and vinegar. Bring to a boil, then reduce the heat and simmer for 2 minutes. Add the tomato puree or sauce and measured water and return to a boil, then gently simmer for 15 minutes.

Meanwhile, place the chipolatas in a small roasting pan and drizzle with a little olive oil. Cook in the oven for 20 minutes.

When the beans and chipolata sausages are near the end of their cooking time, make the dumplings. Place the flour and baking powder in a bowl and season well with salt and pepper. Stir in the herbs. Add the oil and milk and stir lightly with a fork to make a soft dough. With floured hands, roll into 12 dumplings.

Remove the chipolatas from the oven and place in the pan with the beans. Place the dumplings on top and bake in the oven for 25 minutes or until the dumplings are golden and just firm.

*These meatballs are soft, succulent and incredibly moreish. They're also very versatile: they can be served with spaghetti, stuffed in a baked potato, or simply served with a green salad and some bread to mop up the sauce. For a supper party sensation, serve on Creamy Mustard Mash (see page 73) with Cranberry, Red Cabbage & Juniper Jam (see page 180).*

# Soft Beef Kofta Meatballs in Sticky Glaze

### SERVES 4

2 tablespoons olive oil

1 onion, finely chopped

2 garlic cloves, crushed

1½lb lean ground beef

3 cups dairy-free fresh white bread crumbs

1 medium egg, beaten

½ cup dairy-free light cream

good grating of nutmeg

salt and pepper

GLAZE

2 tablespoons all-purpose flour

1¼ cups red wine

2½ cups chicken stock

2 tablespoons syrupy balsamic vinegar

pinch of sugar

Preheat the oven to 400°F.

Heat half the oil in a skillet or sauté pan, add the onion and cook gently for 5 minutes, until softened. Add the garlic and cook for 2 minutes. Remove from heat, transfer to a large bowl and let cool.

Add the ground beef to the cooled onion with the remaining ingredients, season with salt and pepper and mix really well—it's best to use your hands here.

To check that the seasoning is right, fry a little of the mixture in a pan until cooked through and taste, correcting the seasoning if necessary.

Divide the mixture into 24 equal-size balls and place in a roasting pan. Drizzle over the remaining oil and shake to coat in the oil. Roast for 30 minutes, giving the meatballs a shake now and then. Remove from oven, transfer the meatballs to a serving plate and keep warm in the oven on low.

To make the glaze, drain the oil from the roasting pan, reserving 1 tablespoon. Pour the tablespoon of oil back into the roasting pan and place over medium heat on the stove. Sprinkle over the flour, stir well with a wooden spoon and cook out for 2 minutes, scraping all the sediment from the bottom of the pan (this will give it flavor and color).

Add the red wine, stock, and balsamic vinegar and simmer over high heat for 5–10 minutes or until syrupy. Season to taste with salt and pepper and add the sugar.

Strain the sauce over the meatballs and serve.

*Madras curry paste and peanut butter make an excellent base for a hot, nutty sauce. Here they are tossed with sesame noodles, stir-fried vegetables and sizzling beef to make a speedy supper.*

# Nutty Noodles with Wilted Greens & Sticky Beef

## SERVES 4

13oz skirt steak, cut into finger strips

¼ cup syrupy teriyaki sauce

1 teaspoon dried red pepper flakes

12oz medium egg noodles

1 tablespoon sesame oil

1 tablespoon peanut oil

2 large carrots, peeled and cut into strips

1¾ cups finely shredded cavolo nero or collard greens

1 cup podded fresh peas

1 small bunch of cilantro, coarsely chopped

### SAUCE

2 tablespoons Madras curry paste

3 tablespoons crunchy peanut butter (see page 178 for homemade)

1 tablespoon dark soy sauce

1¼ cups coconut milk

pepper

Place the beef strips in a bowl with the teriyaki sauce and red pepper flakes. Mix well to combine and set to one side.

Cook the noodles according to the package instructions, then drain, toss with the sesame oil and set to one side.

Meanwhile, to make the sauce, heat a small saucepan, add the curry paste and cook over medium heat, stirring constantly, for 1 minute. Add the peanut butter, soy sauce, and coconut milk and stir well, then season with pepper. Bring to a boil, then reduce the heat and simmer for 2 minutes.

Heat the peanut oil in a large wok or nonstick skillet over a high heat. Add the beef with all the marinade and stir-fry for 2 minutes. Add the carrots, cavolo nero or collard greens, and peas and stir-fry for another 2 minutes.

Arrange the sesame noodles in 4 warmed serving bowls and divide the stir-fried beef and vegetables on top. Spoon over the peanut sauce and finish with the chopped cilantro. Serve straight away.

*This one-pan dish uses pork tenderloin, as it's lean and tender and great cut into small medallion steaks. It needs to be pan-fried gently to allow all the sugars from the prunes to become sticky and caramelize and make a delicious creamy pan sauce.*

# Pork & Prune Medallions with Creamy Cider & Mustard Sauce

### SERVES 4

1lb pork tenderloin

12 large ready-to-eat prunes, halved

24 small sage leaves

¼ cup all-purpose flour

2 tablespoons olive oil

1 cup hard cider

2–3 teaspoons whole-grain mustard

¼ cup finely grated dairy-free cheddar-style cheese

5 tablespoons dairy-free light cream

salt and pepper

Trim and slice the pork tenderloin on a slant into 12 pieces. Using the palm of your hand, gently flatten the pieces of pork into medallion shapes.

Using a small, sharp knife, cut 2 slits into each medallion. Push half a prune and 2 sage leaves into each cut. Season with pepper.

Place the flour on a plate and season well with salt and pepper. Dust each pork medallion in a little of the seasoned flour.

Heat half the oil in a nonstick skillet, lay in 6 stuffed pork medallions and cook over medium heat for 4–5 minutes on each side, until golden and cooked through. Remove and keep warm. Repeat with the remaining pork medallions.

Splash in the cider and simmer until reduced by half, then stir in the mustard, cheese, and the cream. Season to taste with salt and pepper.

Serve the pork medallions with the sauce, green beans, and roasted new potatoes.

# Weekend Delights

*A stylish, no-cook mezze dish, which is great served with homemade focaccia (see page 138) or dairy-free sourdough. Charentais or cantaloupe melon are good to use, as they're so sweet, juicy, and colorful. Simply take to the table and let everyone tuck in!*

# Melon, Ham & Pine Nut Salad

### SERVES 4

3 large orange bell peppers, halved, cored, and seeded

3 tablespoons extra virgin olive oil

1 small ripe Charentais or cantaloupe melon

12¼ cups arugula leaves

slices of air-cured ham

⅓ cup pine nuts, toasted

1 tablespoon good-quality balsamic vinegar

pepper

Preheat the oven to 425°F. Place the peppers in a roasting pan and drizzle over 1 tablespoon of the olive oil. Roast for 20–25 minutes. Remove from the oven and set to one side to cool.

Cut the melon in half and scoop out the seeds. Cut each half into 4 wedges.

Arrange the melon on a large board and season with pepper. Trickle over the remaining olive oil, then sprinkle with the arugula, roasted peppers, ham, and pine nuts. Finish with a generous grinding of black pepper and drizzle over the balsamic vinegar.

*The classic way to cook asparagus is to steam it, but I rarely do that now, as I love to roast it with just a drizzle of olive oil and a splash of water. It's so easy this way and I think much more delicious.*

# Asparagus with Watercress & Candied Walnut Salad

### SERVES 4

1 cup shelled walnuts

3 tablespoons olive oil

1½ tablespoons sugar

pinch of salt

2 bunches of asparagus, trimmed

1 bunch of watercress, leaves picked

1 tablespoon balsamic vinegar

salt and pepper

¼ cup Smoked Garlic & Chive Mayo (see page 185), to serve

Preheat the oven to 400°F.

To make the candied walnuts, toss the nuts in 1 tablespoon of the oil in a bowl and sprinkle with the sugar and salt. Toss well to coat and transfer to a baking sheet. Place in the oven for 5 minutes. Remove from the oven and give the nuts a shake, then return to the oven for 2–3 minutes or until golden. Set to one side until needed.

Wash the asparagus and place wet in a roasting pan, drizzle with 1 tablespoon of olive oil and season well with salt and pepper. Roast for 6–8 minutes or until just tender.

Place the watercress in a bowl and lightly dress with the balsamic vinegar and the remaining olive oil. Toss in the warm walnuts.

Divide the salad among 4 serving plates and top each with the asparagus. Serve with a dollop of Smoked Garlic & Chive Mayo.

*This is a modern take on a retro starter. Sadly, it could sometimes be ruined by overcooked eggs—the secret is to cook them so that the yolks are just set. Fold into creamy, smoky mayo and layer up with the piquant tapenade, then finish with a top hat of mustard and cress. Serve with plenty of toast and a glass of fizz, but it's also really good just used as a filling to make a tasty sandwich.*

# Vintage Egg Mayo with Tapenade & Cress

### SERVES 4

6 free-range eggs

¼ cup Smoked Garlic & Chive Mayo (see page 185)

3 anchovy fillets, drained

12 large good-quality black ripe olives, pitted

2 tablespoons baby capers, drained

1 pack garden cress

pepper

Place the eggs in a saucepan, cover with cold water and bring to a boil, then reduce the heat and simmer for 3½ minutes.

Immediately remove the eggs from the pan and place in cold water to prevent more cooking. Carefully shell the eggs and coarsely chop—not too finely.

Lightly mix the chopped eggs with the mayo and season to taste with pepper.

Finely chop the anchovies and olives and mix with the capers.

Carefully spoon half the egg mixture into 4 large shot glasses and divide half the anchovy mixture among them. Repeat with another layer of each.

Finish with a mound of cress on each and serve with slices of toasted dairy-free sourdough or rye bread, or Caramelized Onion & Spelt Flatbread (see page 136).

*This is a real showstopper that doesn't require much effort at all. Serve rustic style on a wooden board or much smaller as a canapé. It's perfect for alfresco entertaining—you could even toast the bread on the barbecue and assemble the dish in front of your guests. The oranges and shallots cut through the richness of the smoked trout and avocado.*

# Smoked Trout Bruschetta with Orange & Dill Relish

### SERVES 4–6

⅔ cup dairy-free light cream

1–5 teaspoons dairy-free horseradish sauce

squeeze of lemon juice

13oz skinless smoked trout fillets

1 dairy-free ciabatta-style loaf

2 tablespoons olive oil

pepper

ORANGE & DILL RELISH

2 ripe avocados, halved and pitted

2 oranges, peeled and white pith removed

2 large shallots, finely sliced

2 tablespoons extra virgin olive oil

1 small bunch of dill weed, plus extra sprigs to garnish

salt and pepper

Preheat the oven to 400°F.

Mix together the cream, horseradish, and lemon juice in a large bowl. Season with pepper. Break the trout into large flakes and gently fold into the horseradish mixture. Set to one side.

Cut the loaf in half horizontally and lay both halves on a baking sheet. Drizzle over the olive oil and bake in the oven for 12 minutes, until golden and toasty.

Meanwhile, to make the relish, spoon the avocado flesh out of the shells in dollops. Segment the oranges by cutting between the membranes, catching the juice from one orange and squeezing out any juices remaining in the membrane.

Gently mix together the avocado, orange segments and reserved juice, shallots, extra virgin olive oil, and dill. Season to taste with salt and pepper.

To serve, arrange the loaf halves on a large wooden board. Cut each half into 5. Top each ciabatta slice with the trout mixture. Grind over a little more black pepper and top with the relish and extra dill sprigs. Take to the table and serve.

*This makes a stylish, sophisticated appetizer for six, or a lunch or supper for four. Creamy spinach, smoked salmon, and horseradish make a wonderful flavor combination. If you love poached eggs, try them here—they are a great addition to this dish. Use cold-smoked salmon if you can't get hold of hot-smoked fillets.*

# Hot-smoked Salmon Horseradish Crème with Fresh Spinach Sauce

## SERVES 4–6

2 tablespoons olive oil

2 onions, chopped

2 garlic cloves, crushed

2 potatoes, peeled, halved and thinly sliced (approximately 7½oz prepared weight)

4 cups vegetable stock

4 cups ready-washed spinach leaves

generous grating of nutmeg

6 (3¼oz) pieces of hot-smoked cured salmon fillets

salt and pepper

### TO SERVE

3 tablespoons dairy-free light cream

2–3 teaspoons dairy-free hot horseradish sauce

handful of spinach leaves, finely shredded

Preheat the oven to 400°F.

Heat the oil in a large saucepan and add the onions, then cover with a lid and cook over medium heat, stirring occasionally, for 10 minutes until softened. Add the garlic and potatoes and cook for another 5 minutes.

Add the stock to the pan and bring to a boil, then cover, reduce the heat and simmer for 10 minutes. Add the whole spinach leaves, nutmeg, and salt and pepper to taste, then cook for a minute until the spinach has wilted.

Remove the pan from the heat and let cool a little. Transfer the sauce to a blender or food processor and blend until smooth. Return to a clean saucepan, reheat and check the seasoning.

Place the salmon pieces on a baking sheet and warm through for about 5–6 minutes.

Meanwhile, mix together the cream and horseradish and season to taste with salt and pepper.

Remove the skin from the hot salmon. To serve, simply ladle the sauce into 6 warmed shallow bowls and top with the salmon pieces, horseradish cream, and shredded raw spinach.

*Caramelized pears are given an unusual sweet and sour hit here. The best pears to use are Conference or Concorde, and they don't have to be ripe. They are served here appetizer style, warm with serrano ham and arugula along with crusty bread, but they're equally great served as an accompaniment to roast pork, baked ham, or roast duck.*

# Roasted Salt & Pepper Pears & Serrano Platter

## SERVES 4

6 Conference or Concorde pears

2 teaspoons cracked black pepper

2 tablespoons caster sugar

1 teaspoon sea salt

5 tablespoons cider vinegar

2 tablespoons olive oil

### TO SERVE

2 handfuls of dressed arugula leaves

4oz serrano ham, pastrami, or salt beef

extra virgin olive oil, for drizzling

1 warm crusty loaf

Preheat the oven to 400°F.

Peel and halve the pears (keeping the stalks intact), then lay cut side up in a shallow, nonstick sheet pan.

Place the cracked pepper, sugar, and salt in a small bowl and mix together well. Sprinkle over the pears. Drizzle over the vinegar, oil, and 2 tablespoons water.

Roast for 25 minutes, then remove the pan from the oven, turn the pears over and drizzle over another 3 tablespoons water. Return to the oven for 10–15 minutes, until the pears are golden and just tender.

To serve, place the pears cut side up on a large platter or rustic board. Top with the dressed arugula, tear over the serrano ham, pastrami, or salt beef and drizzle with a little olive oil. Take to the table with a basket of warm bread.

*This fresh, fruity warm salad works perfectly with the rich, crispy duck breast. I was taught many years ago how to get a really crisp skin on duck breast without overcooking the meat. The duck is best served pink and the trick is to let it rest for at least 5 minutes before slicing and arranging on the salad.*

# Duck with Warm Pomegranate, Puy Lentil & Orange Salad

### SERVES 4 AS A APPETIZER

2 small duck breasts, skin on

sea salt, for rubbing

¼ cup dried Puy lentils, washed and cooked according to the package instructions

1 small red onion, finely sliced

1 garlic clove, crushed

3 tablespoons olive oil

seeds of 1 pomegranate

1 large orange, segmented and juice reserved

1 small bunch of flat leaf parsley, coarsely torn

salt and pepper

Preheat the oven to 425°F.

Using a small knife, score the skin of the duck in a lattice fashion and rub each with a little sea salt.

Heat a large skillet over medium heat, add the breasts skin side down and cook for 4 minutes, until really golden, then turn over and sear for another 30 seconds.

Transfer the duck to a wire rack over a roasting pan, skin side up. Roast the duck for 6 minutes. Remove from the oven and let rest in a warm place for 10 minutes.

Meanwhile, mix together the remaining ingredients in a large bowl. Season to taste with salt and pepper.

To serve, arrange the salad on 4 serving plates. Slice the duck into thin slices and arrange on top of the salad. Serve straight away.

*I just love this pie! The pastry is so easy to handle that it doesn't need to be chilled before rolling. The mound of potato and celeriac steams under the pastry crust. It needs at least an hour's cooking, depending on how thinly you slice your potatoes and celeriac, and the end result is crisp and delicious. If celeriac isn't in season, use all potato.*

# Potato & Celeriac Pie with Canola Crust

### SERVES 8

1lb white potatoes, peeled and cut into ¼-inch slices

1 celeriac, peeled and cut into ¼-inch slices

2 large shallots, finely chopped

2 garlic cloves, crushed

2 tablespoons canola oil

1 small bunch of chives, chopped

1 quantity of Soured Cream & Tarragon Dressing (see page 183)

salt and pepper

### PASTRY

4⅔ cups all-purpose flour, plus extra for dusting

pinch of salt

¾ cup canola oil

⅔ cup cold water, plus extra if needed

beaten egg, to glaze

Place the potato and celeriac slices in a large bowl. Add the shallots, garlic, oil, and chives and season really well with salt and pepper. Set to one side for 15 minutes.

Preheat the oven to 400°F. Line a baking sheet with parchment paper.

To make the pastry, sift the flour into a large bowl and stir in the salt. Mix the oil and measured water together in a bowl, then gently mix into the flour mixture to bind the pastry dough together. If too dry, add a little more water.

Roll out one-third of the pastry on a lightly floured surface into a 12-inch circle and place on the lined baking sheet.

Pile on the potato and celeriac mixture, leaving a 1-inch border around the edge. Roll out the remaining pastry into a 14-inch circle and carefully place over the top. Gently press down to seal the edges and roll the edges up to form a thick rim.

Brush the pie with the beaten egg to glaze and bake for 1¼ hours. If getting too dark, reduce the heat to 375°F and cover with a sheet of foil.

Remove the pie from the oven and let cool for a few minutes. Using a serrated knife, carefully cut off the top of the pastry lid.

Spoon the soured cream dressing over the potatoes. Replace the pastry top and let stand for 5 minutes.

Transfer the pie to a serving board. Serve hot, warm, or cold with baked ham, spiced beef, such as pastrami, or smoked salmon.

*This special crab tart is superb with the soy–chili dressing and sesame crust. If fresh crabmeat is tricky to find, you can use fresh cooked shrimp or cooked crayfish tails instead.*

# Crab & Ginger Tart with Soy–chili Dressing

**SERVES 6 AS A MAIN COURSE
OR 12 AS AN APPETIZER**

4-inch piece of fresh ginger root, peeled and coarsely chopped

1 large bunch of flat leaf parsley

2 tablespoons sunflower oil

12oz fresh white crabmeat

2 free-range eggs

2 free-range egg yolks

grated zest of 1 unwaxed lime

1¾ cups dairy-free light cream

### CRUST

2½ cups all-purpose flour, plus extra for dusting

1 teaspoon sea salt

3 tablespoons sesame seeds

⅓ cup extra virgin olive oil

⅓ cup cold water

### DRESSING

4 scallions, finely chopped

juice of 1 lime

1 red chile, finely chopped

3 tablespoons dark soy sauce

6 tablespoons sunflower oil

1 teaspoon sugar

1 tablespoon water

For the crust, mix together the flour, salt, and sesame seeds in a large bowl. Stir in the oil and measured water (you may need slightly less or slightly more water depending on your flour). Using your hands, bring the dough together and form into a flat disk.

Preheat the oven to 400°F.

Roll out the pastry gently on a lightly floured surface and use to line an 11-inch removeable-bottomed tart pan. Cover with plastic wrap and chill in the refrigerator for 15 minutes.

Line the tart shell with parchment paper and half-fill with pie weights. Bake blind for 10–15 minutes. Remove the tart shell from the oven and lift out the paper and weights. Return the tart shell to the oven for another 3–5 minutes, until it is just cooked. Reduce the heat to 375°F.

Place the ginger, parsley, and sunflower oil in a small food processor and blend together into a paste. Spread over the base of the tart shell. Arrange the crabmeat over the top of the ginger paste.

Beat together the eggs, egg yolks, lime zest, and cream in a bowl and season with salt and pepper. Pour into the tart shell. Bake the tart for 30–35 minutes or until just set.

Meanwhile, beat all the dressing ingredients together in a small bowl. Season to taste with salt and pepper.

Serve the tart warm with a drizzling of the soy–chili dressing.

*Named after the clay dish in which it's traditionally cooked, this dish is full of Moroccan flavors. It's all about the spices and the gentle cook, which keeps the chicken moist. You don't need a tagine to make this, just a decent casserole dish with a tight-fitting lid. I serve this with lentils and rice, but couscous can be served instead.*

# Chicken Tagine with Red Lentils & Rice

## SERVES 4

2 tablespoons olive oil

8 skinless chicken thighs

1 garlic clove, crushed

1 tablespoon ground cumin

1 tablespoon coriander seeds, crushed

1 tablespoon sweet smoked paprika

1 onion, sliced

1 (14½oz) can diced tomatoes

1⅔ cups vegetable stock

¾ cup red wine

1¼ cups dried apricots

1 cinnamon stick

2 tablespoons chopped mint

### RED LENTILS & RICE

¾ cup red split lentils, washed

¾ cup basmati rice, washed

2 tablespoons olive oil

juice of ½ lemon, or to taste

Preheat the oven to 350°F.

Rub 1 tablespoon of the olive oil into the chicken thighs. Mix together the garlic, cumin, coriander, and paprika and rub over the chicken thighs on both sides.

Heat a large, nonstick skillet, add the chicken thighs and cook over medium heat for 5 minutes, until golden on both sides. Remove from the pan and set to one side.

Add the remaining oil to the pan and cook the onion for 5 minutes or until softened. Stir in the tomatoes, stock, red wine, apricots, and cinnamon stick and bring to a boil.

Pour the sauce into a casserole dish and place the chicken thighs and any juices on top. Cover with the lid, place in the oven and cook for 1½ hours.

After the tagine has been cooking for an hour, prepare the lentils and rice. Place the lentils in a pan, cover with plenty of cold water and bring to a boil. Reduce the heat and simmer for 15–20 minutes. Drain well.

Meanwhile, cook the basmati rice according to the package instructions, then drain well if necessary.

Toss the cooked lentils and rice together in a bowl and add the olive oil and lemon juice to taste.

Sprinkle the mint over the chicken tagine and serve with the lentils and rice.

*I love baked risotto because you get a combination of soft, creamy rice along with a crisp, baked rice topping. The saffron, orange, and bay flavors infuse into the rice while the chicken roasts on top. I have tried this with small chickens and large chicken joints, but it doesn't work as well, so stick to squab chicken (poussin) for the best results.*

# Saffron-baked Orange Poussin with Crispy-topped Risotto

### SERVES 4

4 single-serve squab chickens (poussins)

4 garlic cloves, crushed

4 bay leaves

1 small bunch of lemon thyme, bruised

3 small oranges, halved

⅔ cup white wine

¼ cup olive oil, plus extra for brushing

about 4 cups chicken stock

2 good pinches of saffron threads

2 large Spanish onions, sliced

2¼ cups risotto rice

salt and pepper

Place the squab chickens in a large glass or ceramic bowl and season well with salt and pepper. Rub over the garlic and sprinkle with the herbs. Squeeze over the juice from the orange halves and add the squeezed halves, then pour in the white wine and half the oil.

Cover the bowl with plastic wrap and let marinate in the refrigerator for 2 hours, or even better overnight.

Preheat the oven to 400°F.

Heat the stock in a saucepan and add the saffron threads. Set to one side.

Heat the remaining oil in a paella pan or large, heavy roasting pan, add the onions and fry for 5 minutes or so, until softened. Stir in the rice and cook for 1 minute.

Place the chickens breast side down on top of the rice and pour over the marinade juices and orange halves and 2½ cups of the stock. Bring to a boil, then cover with foil, transfer to the oven and cook for 25 minutes.

Remove the pan from the oven, turn the chickens over and add the remaining stock. Brush the chickens with a little extra oil and season well with salt and pepper.

Return to the oven, uncovered, and cook for another 30 minutes or until the poussins and rice are cooked. You may need to add extra stock during cooking.

# Roasted Guinea Fowl with Cardamom Bread Sauce

### SERVES 4

2½ cups red wine

1¼ cups ready-to-eat prunes

1 guinea fowl, about 3½lb

4 red onions, cut into 6 wedges

1 teaspoon sugar

1 small bunch of thyme

1 tablespoon olive oil

1 tablespoon balsamic syrup

¼oz bittersweet chocolate

salt and pepper

CARDAMOM BREAD SAUCE

1 large onion, cut into quarters

12 cardamom pods, lightly crushed

12 black peppercorns

1¼ cups almond milk (see page 177 for homemade)

1⅔ cups dairy-free fresh white bread crumbs

¼ cup dairy-free light cream

salt and pepper

Pour the red wine into a bowl, add the prunes and let soak for about 2 hours, then drain.

Preheat the oven to 400°F.

Loosely tie the legs of the guinea fowl with kitchen twine. Season well with salt and pepper and place in a large roasting pan. Arrange the red onions and prunes around the guinea fowl, pour over the wine, sprinkle with the sugar, and top with the thyme. Drizzle over the oil.

Roast the bird for about 1¼ hours until it is dark golden brown and the juices run clear when the thickest part of the thigh is pierced with the tip of a knife. Baste frequently during the cooking time.

Meanwhile, to make the bread sauce, place the onion, cardamom, peppercorns, and almond milk in a saucepan and let infuse for 30 minutes.

Place the pan over low heat and gently bring to a boil. Remove from the heat and strain onto the bread crumbs in a bowl. Beat in the cream and return to the cleaned saucepan. Season well with salt and pepper.

Remove the guinea fowl from the roasting pan and let rest in a warm place for 10 minutes while you finish the sauce.

Reheat the bread sauce, stirring constantly, but do not let it boil. If the sauce becomes too thick, add more milk to obtain a creamy consistency.

Place the roasting pan on the stove, add the balsamic syrup and reduce until syrupy. Stir in the chocolate and season to taste.

Carve the bird. Serve the guinea fowl with a spoonful of the onion, prunes, and juices, and hand round a bowl of the bread sauce.

*With this one-pot wonder, there is no need to seal the meat first or fry off the shallots. All you do is layer up the ingredients in the pan, place on a tight-fitting lid and cook in the oven for 4 hours. Incredibly the lamb caramelizes and everything is ready at the same time. I originally tried this with preserved lemons, but the end result was too overpowering, while the fresh lemons work superbly.*

# Slow-cooked Lamb with Lemon & Oregano

### SERVES 4–6

2 tablespoons extra virgin olive oil

1¾lb waxy new potatoes, washed and thickly sliced

6 banana shallots, peeled but kept whole

1 whole garlic bulb, cut in half across the middle

4 good oregano sprigs

3 bay leaves

2 teaspoons sea salt

1 teaspoon cracked black pepper

about 3½lb (unboned weight) shoulder of lamb, boned

2 small unwaxed lemons, cut into quarters

¾ cup vegetable stock

salt and pepper

Preheat the oven to 325°F.

Pour the oil into a large ovenproof pan and add the potatoes, shallots, garlic, oregano, bay leaves, sea salt, and cracked pepper.

Trim the lamb and cut into 8–10 large chunks. Place in a bowl, squeeze over the juice from the lemon quarters and season with salt and pepper.

Arrange the lamb and squeezed lemon quarters on top of the vegetables and pour over the stock. Cover with a tight-fitting lid and cook in the oven for 3½–4 hours until tender, basting the lamb with the juices occasionally.

To serve, spoon the lamb onto a large warmed plate, top with the potatoes, shallots, garlic, and herbs and spoon over the juices. Serve with green beans and a simple watercress salad.

*Crisp, tender, and succulent all in one mouthful! This is my favorite cut of pork and the end result is wonderful. The cooking temperature may seem high to begin with, but you need that initial blast of heat to get the crackling going—you want it to be good and crispy. If you can, get your butcher to score the belly of pork for you. I love to serve this with baby baked apples or the Roasted Salt & Pepper Pears (see page 116), along with Creamy Mustard Mash (see page 73) and favorite veggies.*

# Salt & Thyme Crusted Pork Belly

### SERVES 4–6

4lb thick end belly of pork

2 tablespoons thyme leaves

1 tablespoon sea salt

pepper

Preheat the oven to 470°F.

Using a really sharp knife, score the skin of the pork with cuts about ½ inch apart. Dry the skin well with paper towels.

Grind together the thyme, sea salt, and a good grinding of pepper in a mortar with a pestle. Using your hands, rub the mixture firmly over the pork skin, getting right into the cuts.

Roast for 45 minutes, then reduce the oven temperature to 325°F and roast for 2½–3 hours more, until the crackling is a deep golden brown and the meat is almost falling apart.

Remove the crackling before carving the meat into thick slices.

*This is a quick pie to make, as it's using lean and tender meat. The dairy-free puff pastry lid is cooked separately while the meat is cooking in a rich juniper and wine sauce.*

# Rich Steak & Venison Pie with a Black Pepper Crust

## SERVES 4

2 tablespoons olive oil

4 red onions, each cut into 8 wedges

9oz sirloin steak, trimmed and cut into ½-inch strips

9oz venison fillet, trimmed and cut into ½-inch strips

1 teaspoon sugar

1 teaspoon all-purpose flour

1¼ cups red wine

1¼ cups chicken stock

3 tablespoons balsamic vinegar

8 juniper berries, lightly crushed

1 bay leaf

3 tablespoons port

salt and pepper

### PASTRY LID

cracked black pepper, for sprinkling

1 sheet store-bought dairy-free puff pastry

beaten egg, to glaze

Heat the oil in a skillet, add the onion wedges and cook gently for 5 minutes. Cover with a lid and cook over low heat for 15–20 minutes, until very soft. Using a slotted spoon, remove from the pan and set to one side.

Add the steak and venison strips to the pan and sear over high heat for 1–2 minutes on each side. Remove from the pan and set to one side.

Return the onions to the pan and stir in the sugar. Sprinkle in the flour and cook gently for 1 minute. Pour in the red wine, stock, and balsamic vinegar, add the juniper berries and bay leaf and bring to a boil. Cook until the liquid has reduced by half and become shiny and slightly sticky.

Meanwhile, preheat the oven to 400°F.

Stir the port into the sauce and season to taste with salt and pepper. Add the meat and then divide among 4 small pie dishes, about 4 inches in diameter.

Sprinkle a board with cracked black pepper. Cut out 4 puff pastry lids slightly larger than the pie dish tops and press lightly on both sides onto the pepper. Cut the top of each lid with a sharp knife to form a lattice pattern, taking care not to cut all the way through the pastry. Brush each with beaten egg to glaze and place on a baking sheet.

Cover each pie dish with foil. Bake the pie filling and pastry lids for 15–20 minutes, until the lids are risen and browned and the filling piping hot.

Top each pie dish with a peppered pastry lid and serve at once.

*This is a deconstructed chili con carne with a real kick, using black beans and roasted in the oven. Don't buy ready-made burgers, as they are so quick and easy to make. A simple tip is to use wet hands for shaping the burgers.*

# Hot Black Bean Sweet Chunky Chili with Steak Burgers & Skinny Fries

### SERVES 4

2 red onions, chopped into chunks

1 large red bell pepper, cored, seeded, and chopped into chunky pieces

2 garlic cloves, unpeeled

¼ cup olive oil

1 (14oz) can black beans, rinsed and drained

10 semidried tomatoes in oil, drained and oil reserved, then chopped

1lb tomatoes, chopped into chunky pieces

2 tablespoons sugar

2 teaspoons dried red pepper flakes

1 teaspoon sea salt

1 teaspoon cracked black pepper

2 tablespoons balsamic vinegar

2 tablespoons cilantro leaves

### SKINNY FRIES

1lb potatoes, washed and cut into thin fries

2 tablespoons olive oil

### BURGERS

1½lb lean ground beef

1 tablespoon olive oil

Preheat the oven to 400°F.

Place the onions, bell pepper, and garlic cloves on a large baking sheet, drizzle with half the oil and roast for 10 minutes.

Meanwhile, toss together the black beans and semidried tomatoes and their oil in a large bowl, season with pepper and set to one side.

Remove the vegetables from the oven. Add the fresh tomatoes and sprinkle with the sugar, red pepper flakes, sea salt, cracked black pepper, and half the balsamic vinegar. Return to the oven and roast for 10–15 minutes more or until the tomatoes look lightly charred.

For the skinny fries, spread the cut potatoes out on a baking sheet lined with parchment paper, drizzle with the oil and toss to coat. Season well with salt and pepper, place in the oven and cook for 20–25 minutes, until golden and crisp.

Meanwhile, make the burgers. Place the ground beef in a bowl, season well with salt and pepper and mix thoroughly with your hands. Divide the mixture into 4 and shape into patties. Set to one side.

Once the roasted vegetables are ready, remove from the oven, mix with the black bean mixture and dress with the remaining oil and balsamic vinegar. Set to one side.

To cook the burgers, heat a ridged grill pan until really hot. Rub the patties all over with the olive oil, add to the hot pan and cook for 3–4 minutes, until lightly charred. Turn over and cook for another 3–4 minutes for medium.

To serve, sprinkle the cilantro over the chili and serve with the burgers and the skinny fries.

# The
# Clean
# Bake

*This soft-textured loaf flavored with meltingly sweet onions is delicious warm from the oven, or toast it for a superb bacon sandwich.*

# Caramelized Onion & Spelt Flatbread

### MAKES 2 LOAVES

2½ cups spelt flour

3¾ cups bread flour, plus extra for dusting

2 teaspoons salt

1 (¼oz) envelope active dry yeast

1⅔ cups warm water

¼ cup olive oil, plus extra for oiling and brushing

2 teaspoons clear honey

sea salt, for sprinkling (optional)

CARAMELIZED ONIONS

2 tablespoons olive oil

2 large onions, finely sliced

Sift the flours into a large bowl and then stir in the salt and yeast. Make a well in the center of the flour mixture. Mix together the measured water, oil, and honey in a bowl, then pour into the well.

Using a flat-bladed knife, draw the flour mixture in from the sides to form a soft dough.

Knead the dough on a lightly floured surface for about 10 minutes, until smooth and elastic.

Place the dough in a lightly oiled large bowl, cover with plastic wrap and let rise in a warm place for about 1 hour or until doubled in size.

Meanwhile, for the caramelized onions, heat the oil in a nonstick skillet and add the onions. Cover with a lid and cook over a very gentle heat for 15 minutes, stirring occasionally. Remove the lid, turn up the heat and cook the onions for another 5 minutes or until lightly golden. Remove from the heat and set to one side to cool.

Tip the risen dough out onto a lightly floured surface and knock back with a firm kneading. Flatten the dough out into a large oval and spoon over the cooled onions. Fold the dough over the onions and knead into the dough until evenly distributed.

Divide the dough in half and roll each piece into a large oval about ½ inch thick. Place each oval on parchment paper and place on a baking sheet.

Make 2 rows of diagonal slashes in each loaf, then open out the slashes to make large holes in the dough. Brush the dough lightly with olive oil, dust with flour and sprinkle with a little sea salt if you desire. Set aside for 10–15 minutes or until the loaves look puffy.

Meanwhile, preheat the oven to 400°F.

Bake the breads for 15–20 minutes, until golden. Remove from the oven and transfer to a wire rack to cool slightly.

The Clean Bake

*There's something about those little dimples of dough filled with olive oil, sprigs of rosemary, and sea salt crystals that just sing summer. This bread really impresses everyone I make it for. It's best eaten warm or on the day that you baked it—don't refrigerate it.*

# Focaccia with Rosemary

## MAKES 2 LOAVES

1oz fresh yeast

1¾ cups warm water

5 cups bread flour, plus extra for dusting

2 teaspoons salt

¼ cup olive oil, plus extra for oiling

TO FINISH

2 tablespoons olive oil

1½ teaspoons coarse sea salt

rosemary sprigs, for sprinkling

Dissolve the yeast in a little of the measured water in a bowl.

Sift the flour into a large bowl and stir in the salt. Make a well in the center of the flour and pour in the yeast mixture along with the oil and the remaining measured water.

Using a flat-bladed knife, draw the flour in from the sides to form a soft dough.

Knead the dough on a lightly floured surface for about 10 minutes until smooth and elastic.

Place the dough in a lightly oiled large bowl, cover with plastic wrap and let rise in a warm place for about 1½ hours or until doubled in size.

Meanwhile, preheat the oven to 425°F.

Tip the risen dough out onto a lightly floured surface and knock back with a firm kneading. Roll it out into 2 long ovals, about 11 inches long. Place on a baking sheet, cover with a clean cloth and let rise until it looks puffy—this will take approximately 15 minutes, depending on the temperature of the room.

When risen, use your fingertips to form dimples in the dough. To finish, brush the dough with the olive oil, sprinkle with the sea salt followed by the rosemary sprigs.

Bake for 10–15 minutes, then reduce the heat to 400°F and bake for another 25–30 minutes, until golden and cooked through. Remove from the oven and transfer to a wire rack to cool slightly.

*This dairy- and gluten-free Mediterranean batter bread is a pantry hero for when friends pop in and you want to impress with an unusual, tasty nibble. Serve torn into strips on a board with some White Bean Creamy Hummus & Dukkah (see page 62). This is also fab served with soups, tagines, and curries.*

# Thyme, Garlic & Chile Socca

## SERVES 4

½ cup gram flour

2 tablespoons chopped thyme leaves

2 garlic cloves, crushed

1 chile, seeded and finely chopped

scant 1 cup water

3 tablespoons olive oil

salt and pepper

Place the flour, thyme, garlic, chile, measured water, 1 tablespoon of the oil, and salt and pepper in a bowl and beat to a smooth batter. Let stand for 30 minutes.

Meanwhile, preheat the oven to 400°F.

Heat a heavy roasting pan or shallow sheet pan in the oven. When really hot, carefully remove from the oven, add 1 tablespoon of the remaining olive oil and swirl to coat the base. Quickly but carefully pour in the batter and return to the oven for 5 minutes.

While the is batter is baking, preheat your broiler to high. After 5 minutes, remove the roasting pan from the oven and drizzle with the remaining olive oil. Place under the broiler for 4–5 minutes or until the batter begins to brown.

Remove the bread from under the broiler, tear into strips and pile on to a warm plate or a board to serve.

*Figs and pepper are the perfect combination. You'll need cracked black pepper for this recipe and not fine black pepper—simply grind it coarsely from the pepper mill and be generous! If you can, eat the bread while it's still warm from the oven.*

# Cracked Black Pepper & Figgy Bread

## SERVES 6

5 cups bread white flour, plus extra for dusting

2 teaspoons cracked black pepper

2 teaspoons salt

1 (¼oz) envelope active dry yeast

1⅔ cups warm water

2 tablespoons olive oil, plus extra for oiling

2 cups ready-to-eat dried figs, coarsely chopped

Sift the flour into a large bowl and then stir in the pepper, salt, and yeast. Make a well in the center of the flour mixture and pour in the measured water and oil.

Using a flat-bladed knife, draw the flour mixture in from the sides to form a soft dough.

Knead the dough on a lightly floured surface for about 10 minutes until smooth and elastic.

Place the dough in a lightly oiled large bowl, cover with plastic wrap and let rise in a warm place for about 1 hour or until doubled in size.

Meanwhile, preheat the oven to 400°F. Lightly flour a baking sheet.

Tip the risen dough out onto a lightly floured surface and knock back with a firm kneading. Flatten the dough out into a large oval and sprinkle with the chopped figs. Fold the dough over the figs and knead into the dough until evenly distributed.

Shape the dough into an oval and place on the prepared baking sheet. Using scissors, roughly slash the top of the loaf.

Bake for 45–50 minutes, until golden. Remove from the oven and transfer to a wire rack to cool slightly.

*Bread doesn't come simpler or quicker than these two recipes!*
*Both are best served warm, straight from the pan.*

# Bacon & Sage Cornbread

## SERVES 4–6

4oz bacon lardons

1 cup all-purpose flour

1 cup instant dried cornmeal

1 tablespoon baking powder

1 tablespoon sugar

1 cup almond milk

2 free-range eggs, beaten

¼ cup canola oil, plus extra for oiling

2 tablespoons chopped sage

2 teaspoons dried red pepper flakes

Preheat the oven to 400°F. Oil an 8-inch square shallow pan and line with parchment paper.

Heat a small skillet, add the lardons and cook until golden. Drain and set aside.

Mix together the flour, cornmeal, baking powder, and sugar in a bowl and season well with salt and pepper. Add all the remaining ingredients, including the lardons, and stir together.

Pour the mixture into the prepared pan and bake for 20 minutes.

Rest the cornbread in the pan for 5 minutes before turning out. Cut into chunks and serve warm.

# Cheese & Chive Soda Bread

## MAKES 12 RUSTIC ROLLS

3⅔ cups all-purpose flour

2 tablespoons baking powder

¼ cup chopped chives

¼ cup mixed seeds, such as pumpkin and sunflower

1 cup finely grated dairy-free cheddar-style cheese

¼ cup olive oil

1¼ cups almond milk (see page 177), plus extra if needed

Preheat the oven to 425°F. Line a baking sheet with parchment paper.

Sift the flour and baking powder into a large bowl and season well with salt and pepper. Add the chives, seeds, and cheese and mix well.

Combine the oil and milk in a pitcher, then gently mix in to the flour mixture to form a soft dough, adding extra milk if necessary.

Divide the dough into 12 even-size pieces and roll each into a ball on a lightly floured surface. Arrange the dough balls on the lined baking sheet. Bake for 25 minutes, until puffed and golden. Serve warm.

*These breadsticks are perfect for dipping into creamy hummus
(see page 160 for homemade). I also like to wrap them with
air-cured ham to serve as a posh nibble.*

# Poppy Seed Grissini

### MAKES ABOUT 32

1⅔ cups bread flour,
plus extra for dusting

1 (¼oz) envelope active dry yeast

1 teaspoon salt

1¼ cups warm water

3 tablespoons olive oil

beaten egg, to glaze

3 tablespoons poppy seeds

Sift the flour into a large bowl and then stir in the yeast and salt. Make a well in the center of the flour mixture and pour in the measured water and oil.

Using a flat-bladed knife, draw the flour mixture in from the sides to form a firm but slightly sticky dough.

Knead the dough on a lightly floured surface for about 10 minutes, until smooth and elastic.

Place the dough in a large clean bowl, cover with plastic wrap and let rest for 30 minutes.

Put the dough on a lightly floured surface and knead for another 10 minutes.

Meanwhile, preheat the oven to 400°F, and lightly flour 2 large baking sheets.

Roll and shape the dough into a rectangle about 8 inches x 12 inches and ½ inch thick. Cut the rectangle into 4 quarters, then cut each quarter into 8 equal strips. Stretch each strip to about 8 inches in length.

Place the strips on the prepared baking sheets about ¾ inch apart, brush with beaten egg to glaze and sprinkle with the poppy seeds.

Bake the breadsticks for 15–18 minutes, until golden and firm. Remove from the oven and transfer to a wire rack to cool.

*I first tried this at a dairy-intolerant friend's birthday party. I couldn't believe how light, moist, and deliciously rich a layer cake could be. It's so easy to make and you can change the flavor of the cake by adding lemon or orange zest, coffee, or almond extract. However, my favorite version has to be this classic vanilla bean-flavored one, filled with strawberry preserves.*

# Vanilla Bean & Olive Oil Layer Cake

### SERVES 8

5 free-range eggs

¾ cup superfine sugar

pinch of salt

2 teaspoons vanilla bean paste

¾ cup olive oil

1 cup all-purpose flour

1½ teaspoons baking powder

¼ cup strawberry preserves

vanilla sugar, for sprinkling

TO SERVE

raspberries or strawberries

dairy-free cream

Preheat the oven to 375°F. Line the bottom of 2 x 8-inch layer cake pans with parchment paper.

Place the eggs and sugar in a large bowl and, using a hand-held electric mixer, beat until thick and mousse-like. Add the salt and vanilla bean paste.

Beat in the oil in a steady stream, then sift in the flour and baking powder and quickly fold in.

Spoon the batter into the prepared pans and bake for 25 minutes until pale golden and just firm.

Let cool in the pans for 5 minutes. They will fall slightly while cooling, but don't panic—this is normal. Remove from the pans and let cool on a wire rack.

Sandwich the cakes together with the preserves and place on a serving plate. Sprinkle the top with vanilla sugar and serve with a pile of fresh, sweet raspberries or strawberries and a pitcher of dairy-free cream.

*Oh my goodness, these moreish muffin-type cakes are wonderfully light and so, so moist! These are fabulous simply served straight from the oven, or let them cool and top with dairy-free cream cheese frosting as below.*

# Carrot & Walnut Muffelettas

### MAKES 16

1¾ cups all-purpose flour

3¾ teaspoons baking powder

1 cup dairy-free spread

4 free-range eggs

generous 1 cup superfine sugar

grated zest of 1 large orange

¾ cup coarsely shredded carrot (about 1 large carrot)

1 cup walnuts, coarsely chopped

### FROSTING

1 cup dairy-free cream cheese

1 tablespoon confectioners' sugar, sifted, or to taste

ground cinnamon, for sprinkling

Preheat the oven to 375°F. Line 8 sections of a muffin pan with paper bake cups.

Place all the ingredients except the walnuts in a food processor and process until well mixed.

Add the walnuts and pulse until well combined.

Fill the paper cups about half full with the batter and bake for 18 minutes or until golden and just firm.

Meanwhile, to make the frosting, mix together the cream cheese and confectioners' sugar in a bowl.

Remove the muffelettas from the oven and let cool a little. Top each with the frosting and sprinkle each with a little ground cinnamon.

*These are grown-up cupcakes—dark chocolate with a hit of lime, topped with a glossy fondant chili chocolate sauce. They take no time at all to bake, but don't forget them, as you want them to be a little bit squidgy in the center.*

# Lime Chocolate Cupcakes with Chili Fondant Sauce

### MAKES 8

⅔ cup dairy-free spread, plus extra for greasing

¾ cup superfine sugar

grated zest of 1 unwaxed lime

2 large free-range eggs, beaten

1 cup all-purpose flour

1 teaspoon baking powder

½ cup dairy-free unsweetened cocoa powder

3 tablespoons hazelnut milk

CHILI FONDANT SAUCE

3 tablespoons light corn syrup

3½oz dairy-free semisweet chocolate, broken into pieces

1–2 teaspoons Tabasco sauce, to taste

1 tablespoon finely chopped pistachio nuts (optional)

Preheat the oven to 400°F. Grease 8 section of a large, nonstick muffin pan.

Place the spread, sugar, and lime zest in a food processor and blend together until pale and creamy. With the food processor running, gradually add the eggs. Sift together the flour, baking powder, and cocoa. Add to the processor with the hazelnut milk and pulse briefly until just mixed in.

Spoon the batter into the prepared muffin sections and bake for about 10–12 minutes, until just firm but still squidgy in the center.

Meanwhile, for the sauce, place the corn syrup and chocolate in a small saucepan over low heat and stir until melted and smooth. Add the Tabasco sauce to taste. Set aside to cool.

Remove the cupcakes from the oven and let cool in the pan for 5 minutes, then transfer to a wire rack.

Place the cupcakes on a serving plate and top each with the cooled fondant. Sprinkle with the pistachios, if using, and serve.

*These Cinnamon & Orange Cookies are the perfect spiced bites to enjoy with your coffee. The Cocoa Crumble Cookies (see below) are rich in cocoa, not too sweet, and best served on the day of baking.*

# Cinnamon & Orange Cookies

### MAKES 20

½ cup dairy-free spread

¼ cup firmly packed light brown sugar

1¼ cups all-purpose flour, plus extra for dusting

1¼ teaspoons baking powder

1 tablespoon ground cinnamon

grated zest of 1 orange

sifted confectioners' sugar, for dusting

Preheat the oven to 375°F. Lightly flour 2 cookie sheets.

Beat together the spread and sugar in a bowl until light and fluffy. Sift in the flour, baking powder, and cinnamon, add the orange zest and mix well.

Divide the dough into 20, roll with your hands into balls and place on the prepared cookie sheets. Flatten the cookies with a wet fork.

Bake for 15 minutes. Remove from the oven and let cool slightly on the sheets before transferring to a wire rack. Dust with confectioners' sugar and serve warm or cold.

# Cocoa Crumble Cookies

### MAKES 10

½ cup dairy-free spread

⅓ cup superfine sugar

1 cup all-purpose flour, plus extra for dusting

1 teaspoon baking powder

¼ cup dairy-free unsweetened cocoa powder, plus extra for dusting

3¼oz dairy-free semisweet chocolate, coarsely chopped

Beat together the spread and sugar in a bowl until light and fluffy. Sift in the flour, baking powder, and cocoa and mix well, then stir in the chopped chocolate. Roll the dough into a thick cylinder, wrap in plastic wrap and chill in the refrigerator for 1 hour.

Meanwhile, preheat the oven to 375°F. Line 2 cookie sheets with parchment paper.

Cut the dough into 10 slices and place on the prepared cookie sheets. Flatten the cookies with the back of a floured fork.

Bake for 18–20 minutes. Remove from the oven and let cool on the sheets for 10 minutes before transferring to a wire rack. Dust with cocoa to serve.

*This deliciously moist coconut cake is also wheat free. Serve as a teatime cake, or for a sophisticated dessert, serve with a fruit salad, as here, or just raspberries or mango, or with a lemon sorbet.*

# Coconut & Lime Cake

### SERVES 8–10

3 cups unsweetened shredded coconut

1 cup dairy-free spread, softened, plus extra for greasing

generous 1 cup superfine sugar

grated zest and juice of 2 unwaxed limes

3 free-range eggs, beaten

¾ cup rice flour

1½ teaspoons gluten-free baking powder

¼ cup confectioners' sugar

### FRUIT SALAD

4 passion fruit, halved and seeds and juice scooped out

1 large mango, pitted, peeled, and cut into chunks

grated zest of 1 unwaxed lime

Preheat the oven to 325°F. Lightly grease and flour a 9-inch round springform cake pan.

Place the coconut in a food processor and process for about 2 minutes until fine in texture. Remove and set to one side.

Add the spread, superfine sugar, and lime zest to the food processor and blend until pale and creamy. Gradually add the eggs, pulsing the machine constantly. Pulse in the coconut, rice flour, and baking powder until well mixed.

Spoon into the prepared pan and level the top with the back of a spoon. Bake for about 45 minutes or until lightly golden and just firm.

Meanwhile, place the lime juice in a small bowl, sift in the confectioners' sugar and mix well.

Remove the cake from oven and let cool for 10 minutes. Spoon over the lime mixture and let cool in the pan for 20 minutes.

Remove the cake from the pan and place on a serving plate.

For the fruit salad, combine the passion fruit, mango, and lime zest in a serving bowl and serve with the cake.

# Desserts

*A bubbling hot, upside-down banana toffee extravaganza! A touch of sea salt in this sweet, sticky dessert really works. Classic tarte tatin is made with caramelized apples and a sweet shortcrust pastry, but for this cheats' version, ready-made dairy-free puff pastry works best.*

# Salted Caramel Banana Toffee Tatin

### SERVES 6

3 tablespoons canola oil

⅓ cup firmly packed light brown sugar

good pinch of sea salt

7 medium bananas, cut into 1-inch thick slices

12oz store-bought dairy-free puff pastry

all-purpose flour, for dusting

2 limes, cut into wedges

Preheat the oven to 400°F.

Heat the oil and sugar in a 10-inch nonstick, ovenproof skillet and simmer for 2 minutes, until well dissolved and bubbling hot—it will slightly separate, but do not panic. Sprinkle in the salt.

Carefully place the banana slices in the pan on top of the caramel in a single layer, making sure they are tightly pushed together.

Roll out the pastry on a lightly floured surface to form a square. Using a sharp knife, cut out a circle slightly larger than the pan. Lift the pastry over the bananas like a blanket, allowing the edges to fall into the side.

Place the pan on a cookie sheet and bake for about 35 minutes, until bubbling hot and the puff pastry is golden and cooked.

To serve, remove from the oven and let stand for 4–5 minutes before carefully turning out onto a large serving plate with the bananas facing up. Serve with the lime wedges for squeezing over.

*Rice pudding is one of my favorite comfort puddings of all time. This is made all the more special by the addition of coconut cream and zesty lime. Serve with griddled pineapple or a dollop of homemade Rhubarb & Vanilla Jam or the Summer Pudding Jam (see opposite).*

# Coconut Rice Pudding with Grilled Pineapple

### SERVES 4

generous 1 cup shortgrain rice, washed

2 cups water

1¼ cups coconut cream

⅔ cup granulated sugar

grated zest of 1 unwaxed lime

1 small pineapple, skin removed, cored, and cut into small wedges

1 tablespoon small mint leaves

Place the rice and measured water in a saucepan over medium heat and bring to a boil. Cover with a lid and reduce the heat to low. Cook for 10–12 minutes or until the water has been absorbed and the rice is almost cooked—add a little extra water if needed.

Stir in the coconut cream, sugar, and lime zest, replace the lid on the pan and continue cooking over low heat, stirring occasionally, for 10–12 minutes, until thick, creamy, and cooked.

Meanwhile, heat a ridged grill pan over high heat, add the pineapple wedges and cook for a few minutes on each side or until caramelized.

To serve, spoon the rice into warmed serving bowls, top each with the hot grilled pineapple and sprinkle with a few small mint leaves.

*This Summer Pudding Jam goes well with the Meringue Nougats (see page 159), while the Rhubarb & Vanilla Jam (see below) is perfect with scones or stirred into porridge for a breakfast treat.*

# Summer Pudding Jam

### SERVES 6

juice of 1 orange

⅓ cup granulated sugar

1½ cups raspberries

1 cup blackberries, black currants, or red currants

2¼ cups strawberries, hulled and halved if large

Place the orange juice and sugar in a shallow pan. Heat over medium heat until the sugar has dissolved, then bring to a boil and reduce by half.

Add 1 cup of the raspberries and crush with a masher. Cook until syrupy, jammy, and sticky.

Add the blackberries or currants and toss in the hot sauce for 2 minutes, then add the strawberries and remaining raspberries and toss in the hot sauce.

Pour out onto a large tray and let cool, then spoon into a sterilized jar. Keep in the refrigerator and eat within 3–4 days.

---

# Rhubarb & Vanilla Jam

### MAKES ONE 1 QUART

2lb rhubarb, trimmed and cut into 1¼-inch lengths

1kg (2lb) jam sugar

juice of 1 lemon

grated zest of 1 orange

1 vanilla bean, split

Place the rhubarb and sugar in a preserving pan or wok and heat over low heat until all the sugar has dissolved.

Add the remaining ingredients and stir well. Turn up the heat and bring to a boil. Use a spoon to skim the surface, then allow the jam to boil rapidly for 10–15 minutes. To test the consistency of jam, place a couple of saucers in the freezer. Spoon a little of the jam onto a chilled saucer and allow to cool slightly, then run your finger through it—it should wrinkle slightly.

Carefully pour into a sterilized 1-quart Kilner or other preserving jar, removing the vanilla bean, and seal straight away, then set to one side to cool. Keep in a cool, dark place for up to 3 months. Once opened, keep in the refrigerator.

*Full of flavor, juicy, and sweet, these nectarines are my modern take on peach melba. They can be served with the Meringue Nougats (see below), or with dairy-free icecream.*

# Roasted Vanilla Nectarines with Sweet Wine & Berry Sauce

## SERVES 4–6

⅔ cup granulated sugar

½ vanilla bean, split and seeds scraped out

6 ripe nectarines, halved and pitted

grated zest and juice of 1 large orange

7 tablespoons sweet dessert wine

1 cup blackberries

1 cup raspberries, mixed with 1 tablespoon water

Preheat the oven to 400°F.

Mix together the sugar and the vanilla seeds and pod in a bowl.

Place the nectarines in a roasting pan and sprinkle with the vanilla sugar. Pour over the orange zest and juice and 5 tablespoons of the wine. Roast the nectarines for 30 minutes until just soft.

Turn the nectarines into a colander over a bowl to collect any juices. Let cool for a few minutes before transferring to a serving dish.

Add the juices from the nectarines and remaining wine to a shallow pan, bring to a boil and reduce to 4 tablespoons. Add the berries and cook for 30 seconds, then spoon the berry sauce over the nectarines.

# Meringue Nougats

## SERVES 4

4 egg whites

generous 1 cup superfine sugar

2 teaspoons cornstarch

2 teaspoons white wine vinegar

2 cups sliced almonds, toasted

1 vanilla bean, split and seeds scraped out

Preheat the oven to 285°F. Line 2 baking sheets with parchment paper.

Beat the egg whites in a large bowl until stiff. Beat in the sugar, 1 tablespoon at a time, until it is all incorporated and the mixture is stiff enough to stand a spoon up in. Fold in the cornstarch, vinegar, almonds, and the scraped-out vanilla seeds.

Using 2 tablespoons, roughly mold 12 oval-shaped meringues onto the baking sheets. Bake for about 35 minutes. When cooked, remove from the oven and let cool. Keep in an airtight container until needed.

*This mousse is very rich and creamy and you won't be disappointed. The secret ingredient, although you'd never guess, are prunes—dried plums. Serve it with chopped pistachios and plenty of grated chocolate.*

# Plummy Chocolate Mousse with Pistachios

### SERVES 4–6

1 cup ready-to-eat vanilla prunes

¾ cup water

2 tablespoons brandy (optional)

4oz dairy-free semisweet chocolate, broken into pieces, plus extra for grating

3 egg whites

4 teaspoons superfine sugar

2 tablespoons pistachio nuts, coarsely chopped

Place the prunes in a saucepan and add the measured water to barely cover them. Simmer gently for about 15 minutes, until very, very soft.

Transfer to a small food processor with any remaining cooking liquid and the brandy, if using, and blend to a smooth puree.

Place the chocolate in a small heatproof bowl over a saucepan of gently simmering water and stir with a spatula until the chocolate has melted. Remove from the heat and let cool for 5 minutes.

Beat the egg whites in a large bowl until just stiff, then add the sugar and beat again until thick and glossy.

Stir the melted chocolate into the prune puree and beat together well.

Using a large metal spoon, quickly stir a spoonful of the beaten egg white into the chocolate mixture—this will help to loosen the mixture. Add the remaining egg whites to the mixture and fold in.

Spoon the mousse into 4 or 6 medium-size espresso cups and chill for at least 1 hour. Sprinkle with the pistachios and some grated chocolate just before serving.

*Scrumptious and moist, this cake is also very versatile, as you can change the fruits as the seasons go by—this version with rhubarb is good for spring, while plump gooseberries are lovely in summer, halved and pitted plums in the fall and peeled, cored, and sliced pears in winter. Delicious served warm with Homemade Custard Sauce flavored with cardamom (see page 169). Any leftovers can be served with afternoon tea.*

# Rhubarb, Almond & Orange Pudding Cake

## SERVES 6

canola oil, for oiling

1 cup dairy-free spread

generous 1 cup superfine sugar, plus extra for sprinkling

3 free-range eggs, beaten

1¾ cups ground almonds

⅔ cup instant dried cornmeal

1 teaspoon baking powder

grated zest of 2 oranges

9oz rhubarb, trimmed and cut into 3-inch thin sticks

Preheat the oven to 375°F. Lightly oil a 9-inch round, nonstick springform or sponge cake pan and line the bottom and side with parchment paper.

Place the spread and sugar in a food processor and blend together until pale and creamy. With the food processor running, gradually add the eggs.

Mix together the ground almonds, cornmeal, baking powder, and orange zest, add to the processor and pulse briefly to combine.

Spoon the batter into the prepared cake pan and lay the rhubarb sticks on the surface like the spokes of a wheel. Sprinkle with a little extra superfine sugar and bake for about 1 hour, until firm and golden.

Let the cake stand for 20 minutes before serving.

*What could be more heavenly than an oozy, saucy chocolate pudding? This is good enough to serve for any occasion—straight from the oven with the orange-flavored coconut cream, as the longer you leave it sitting, the less saucy it becomes.*

# Mega Saucy Chocolate Pud with Orange Coconut Cream

### SERVES 6–8

7 tablespoons dairy-free spread, plus extra for greasing

1 cup granulated sugar

2 free-range eggs, beaten

⅔ cup dairy-free milk

1½ cups all-purpose flour

1½ teaspoons baking powder

¼ cup dairy-free unsweetened cocoa powder

### TOPPING

¾ cup firmly packed light brown sugar

¾ cup dairy-free unsweetened cocoa powder, sifted

2½ cups very hot water

### COCONUT CREAM

1 (12oz) can full-fat coconut milk, chilled in the refrigerator overnight or for 24 hours

grated zest of 1 orange

Preheat the oven to 375°F. Lightly grease a shallow, ovenproof dish about 2 quarts in capacity.

Beat together the spread and granulated sugar in a bowl until light and fluffy. Add the eggs and milk and beat well. Sift in the flour, baking powder, and cocoa powder and fold in until combined. Spread the mixture into the prepared dish.

For the topping, mix together the brown sugar and cocoa powder and sprinkle over the pudding mixture. Gently pour over the measured water to cover and bake for about 35–40 minutes or until the pudding has risen and is just set but still really saucy.

Meanwhile, open the chilled can of coconut milk. Scoop the coconut cream that has solidified at the top of the can into a bowl, leaving behind the watery liquid at the bottom. Add the orange zest to the bowl and beat briefly until lightly whipped.

Serve the hot pudding straight away with the coconut cream.

*Ice cream in a whiz! Serve in cornets or in coupes with a wafer, or fab with the Roasted Vanilla Nectarines with Sweet Wine & Berry Sauce (see page 168). Ready-frozen fruits can be used instead of frozen fresh ones, but the end result will never be as good.*

# Raspberry & Banana Instant Ice Cream

### SERVES 4

2 ripe bananas

1¾ cups fresh raspberries, frozen

3 tablespoons dairy-free light cream

3 tablespoons confectioners' sugar

Peel and roughly chop the bananas, then place in the freezer for 1 hour or until semi-frozen.

Add the frozen banana with the raspberries to a food processor and blend until just smooth.

Add the cream and sugar and pulse until combined.

Serve straight away, or scrape into a freezerproof container and freeze until needed.

*An apple pie with attitude, the rosemary and cider really make this trad pie something else. As the cornmeal pastry crust cooks, it molds itself over the apple halves. The final sprinkling of granulated sugar is essential as it creates a lovely crust. Serve with Homemade Custard Sauce or Vanilla Ice Cream (see opposite).*

# Cider Baked Apple Pie
# with Cornmeal Pastry

### SERVES 6

1 cup plus 2 tablespoons all-purpose flour, plus extra for dusting

⅓ cup instant dried cornmeal

pinch of salt

7 tablespoons dairy-free spread

1 large egg, beaten

about 1–2 tablespoons cold water

granulated sugar, for sprinkling

FILLING

6 large dessert apples, peeled, cored, and halved

⅔ cup hard cider

¼ cup firmly packed light brown sugar

1 rosemary sprig

Preheat the oven to 400°F.

Sift the flour into a bowl and stir in the cornmeal and salt. Add the spread in small pieces and lightly blend in with your fingertips until the mixture resembles fine bread crumbs. Alternatively, place the ingredients in a food processor and blend together. Gently mix in the egg and enough of the measured water to bind the pastry dough together. Wrap in plastic wrpa and chill in the refrigerator for 30 minutes.

Place the apples cut side down in a shallow, round dish about 9 inches in diameter. Pour the cider over the apples, then sprinkle with the brown sugar and tuck in the rosemary sprig.

Roll out the pastry on a lightly floured surface until it is large enough to lay over the apples as a blanket. Carefully lift the pastry over the apples, trim the edge and tuck inside the dish. Lightly sprinkle the pastry with the granulated sugar.

Bake the pie for 40–45 minutes, until the apples are softened and cooked and the pastry crust is golden and crisp.

*Nothing beats homemade custard. The flavoring for this*
*recipe is traditional vanilla but various other infusions can*
*be used instead, such as grated orange zest, rosemary sprigs,*
*or a handful of crushed cardamom seeds.*

# Homemade Custard Sauce

### SERVES 4

1¾ cups almond milk
(see page 177 for homemade)

1 vanilla bean, split

4 egg yolks

3 tablespoons granulated sugar

2 teaspoons cornstarch

¼ cup dairy-free light cream

Heat the almond milk with the vanilla bean in a saucepan and very gently bring to the boil. Remove from the heat and let infuse for 10 minutes.

Beat together the egg yolks, sugar, and cornstarch in a bowl.

Gradually pour the infused milk onto the egg yolk mixture, stirring constantly. Strain the mixture through a fine-mesh strainer, removing the vanilla bean, back into the cleaned pan.

Return the pan to very low heat and stir constantly until the mixture thickens enough to coat the back of a spoon, but do not allow to boil.

Strain through a strainer into a clean bowl and stir in the cream.

*Vanilla Ice Cream*
To turn this recipe into a simple ice cream, allow the custard to cool and add 2 tablespoons sifted confectioners' sugar before pouring into an ice cream maker and churning according to the manufacturer's instructions. Alternatively, turn into a shallow freezerproof dish, cover and freeze for about 4–6 hours, until just frozen. Remove from the freezer and process in a food processor until smooth. Return to the freezer until needed.

*Frangipane is a term used for a rich almond paste, but in this recipe ground walnuts are used instead of almonds: simply place walnut pieces in a food processor and process until fine. The walnut paste makes a perfect base for the plums to stick to and keeps everything moist. Adding rice flour gives the pastry a lovely shortbread texture.*

# Frangipane Plum Tart

## SERVES A GENEROUS 6!

1½lb plums, halved, pitted, and each half cut into 4

sifted confectioners' sugar, for dusting

### PASTRY

2 cups all-purpose flour, plus extra for dusting

½ cup rice flour

¾ cup dairy-free spread

¼ cup granulated sugar

grated zest of 1 orange

1 large egg, beaten

1–2 tablespoons cold water

### FRANGIPANE

7 tablespoons dairy-free spread

½ cup granulated sugar

1 egg and 1 egg yolk, beaten together

2 tablespoons all-purpose flour

1 cup ground walnuts

Preheat the oven to 400°F. Line a large cookie sheet with parchment paper and dust with a little flour.

To make the pastry, sift the flours into a bowl. Add the spread in small pieces and lightly blend in with your fingertips until the mixture resembles fine bread crumbs. Alternatively, place the ingredients in a food processor and blend together. Stir in the sugar and orange zest. Gently mix in the egg and enough of the measured water to bind the pastry dough together. Wrap in plastic wrap and chill in the refrigerator for 30 minutes.

Roll out the pastry on a lightly floured surface to a small rectangle. Continue to roll very thinly into a rectangle about 9½ x 14 inches. Transfer to the prepared cookie sheet.

For the frangipane, beat together the spread and sugar in a bowl until light and fluffy. Add the eggs a little at a time, beating well between each addition. Fold in the flour and walnuts.

Using a flat-bladed knife, carefully spread the frangipane in a thin, even layer to cover the pastry base, leaving a ½-inch border around the edges.

Arrange the plums evenly in 5 rows and lightly push them into the frangipane.

Bake for 30–35 minutes or until the frangipane is just firm, the pastry golden, and the plums bubbling hot.

To serve, dust with confectioners' sugar and slide the tart on the paper on to a large serving board.

*Serve these little pots of soft Lemon Posset with Cocoa Crumble Cookies or Cinnamon & Orange Cookies (see page 148). The Sparkling Jellies (below) are simply delicious. You can use any sparkling wine, but for special occasions I like to use Champagne.*

# Lemon Posset with Strawberries

1⅔ cups canned coconut milk

3 tablespoons granulated sugar

grated zest from 1 unwaxed lemon and juice from ½

4 teaspoons cornstarch

2 tablespoons cold water

1¼ cups strawberries, hulled and sliced

sifted confectioners' sugar, for dusting

Pour the coconut milk into a small saucepan and add the sugar and lemon zest. Place over medium heat and simmer until the sugar has dissolved.

Dissolve the cornstarch in the measured water in a small bowl. Stir the cornstarch mixture into the coconut milk and simmer, stirring, for 1 minute. Stir in the lemon juice and let cool slightly.

Pour the posset into 4 small Kilner or other preserving jars, or tumblers. Chill in the refrigerator for 2 hours or until just set. To serve, top each with the strawberries and dust well with confectioners' sugar.

# Sparkling Jellies

MAKES 4

3 sheets of leaf gelatin

2 tablespoons granulated sugar

1¾ cups sparkling wine

1 cup blueberries

1 cup raspberries

¼ cup small seeded red grapes

Soak the gelatin sheets in a bowl of cold water for 5 minutes.

Meanwhile, place the sugar and ½ cup of the sparkling wine in a saucepan and stir over very low heat until the sugar has dissolved. Pour into a large pitcher.

Squeeze the gelatin leaves to remove the excess water, then stir them into the warm liquid. Stir in the remaining sparkling wine.

Divide the berries and grapes among 4 glasses. Pour in the wine mixture to just cover. Place the glasses in the refrigerator and leave for about 2 hours or until just set. Serve straight away—the longer the jelly is out of the refrigerator, the more it will soften.

*Serve this flourless, rich cake with espresso syrup and a sprinkling of raspberries for a sophisticated chocolate dessert. Strong coffee and chocolate just go hand in hand—it's one of the best flavor combinations I know—and the addition of cornmeal gives the cake a unique texture. This cake will keep for at least a week if stored in the refrigerator.*

# Chocolate Cornmeal Cake with Espresso Syrup

### SERVES 8

canola oil, for oiling

7oz dairy-free semisweet chocolate, broken into pieces

1 cup dairy-free spread

generous 1 cup superfine sugar

3 free-range eggs, beaten

1¾ cups ground almonds

½ cup instant dried cornmeal

1 teaspoon baking powder

⅓ cup dairy-free unsweetened cocoa powder, sifted

### TO FINISH

2 cups strong coffee or instant espresso

generous ¾ cup superfine sugar

sifted confectioners' sugar, for dusting

raspberries, to serve

Preheat the oven to 350°F. Lightly oil an 11-inch round, nonstick springform cake pan and line the base with parchment paper.

Place the chocolate in a heatproof bowl over a saucepan of gently simmering water and stir with a spatula until the chocolate has melted. Remove from the heat and let cool for 5 minutes.

Beat together the spread and sugar in a bowl until light and fluffy. Add the eggs a little at a time, beating well between each addition. Fold in the almonds, cornmeal, baking powder, and cocoa, then gently stir in the melted chocolate.

Spoon the mixture into the prepared pan and bake for about 30–35 minutes or until just firm.

Remove the cake from the oven and prick the surface with a toothpick. Spoon ⅓ cup of the coffee over the surface of the cake and let cool for 45 minutes before removing from the pan.

Place the remaining coffee in a small saucepan, add the superfine sugar and simmer for about 5 minutes, until syrupy. Let cool slightly.

Remove the lining paper from the cake and place the cake on a serving plate. Dust with confectioners' sugar. To plate up restaurant style, using a large hot knife (dipped in boiling water), cut the cake into neat wedges, place on medium-size plates and sit a small pile of raspberries to the side, then drizzle over a little of the coffee syrup. Or to serve family style, take the cake to the table with a bowl of raspberries and a pitcher of the warm coffee syrup.

*This is a delicious, squidgier version of that family favorite tiffin cake. It's great served as a teatime treat, or cut into smaller pieces and serve with after-dinner coffee. You can replace the apricots with raisins, figs, dates, cherries, or whichever is your favorite. For an adult version, add a slug of brandy.*

# Chocolate & Apricot Fudgy Refrigerator Cake

## MAKES 16 SQUARES

10 tablespoons dairy-free spread

5 tablespoons light corn syrup

2 tablespoons dairy-free unsweetened cocoa powder, sifted

1¼ cups dried apricots, finely chopped

2 nuggets of stem ginger, finely chopped

3¼oz dairy-free semisweet chocolate, broken into chunks

7oz dairy-free Graham crackers

Line an 8-inch square pan with parchment paper.

Place the spread, corn syrup, and cocoa powder in a deep saucepan over medium heat and mix well. Gently bring to a boil and let bubble gently for 2 minutes.

Stir in the apricots and ginger, return to a boil and mix well.

Take the pan off the heat and stir in the chocolate.

Place half the Graham crackers in a plastic bag and beat with a rolling pin until fine crumbs, then stir into the mixture.

Place the remaining crackers in a plastic bag and bash until gently broken into chunks, then stir into the mixture.

Spoon the mixture into the prepared pan and level out. Set aside to cool for 30 minutes.

Run a fork over the top to make it less smooth. Place in the refrigerator for 4 hours (or overnight, if possible) to set before cutting into squares.

# Basics

*Almond milk is now available in most supermarkets and health food stores, but making your own is pretty simple—you just need to soak the almonds for at least 1–2 days. The longer you soak the nuts, the creamier and more flavorsome your milk will become.*

# DIY Fresh Almond Milk

## MAKES 2 CUPS

1 cup raw almonds

2 cups water

maple syrup, vanilla extract, or honey, to taste (optional)

Place the almonds in a bowl and cover with cold water. Leave to soak for 1–2 days.

Drain the almonds and rinse well.

Place the almonds and the measured water in a blender and pulse to break the almonds up. Blend vigorously for 2–3 minutes or until smooth and creamy.

Line a strainer with a piece of cheesecloth. Strain the almond milk through the lined strainer into a pitcher and squeeze out any excess.

Cover the pitcher with plastic wrap and place in the refrigerator. It will last for up to 2 days and can be sweetened to taste with maple syrup, vanilla extract, or honey.

*This homemade Cashew Honey Cream is thick and tasty—try it with the Salted Caramel Banana Toffee Tatin (see page 154), on scones or with fresh fruit. Instead of honey, you can add a hit of vanilla bean paste or drizzle of maple syrup for flavor. Crunchy or creamy, the Instant Peanut Butter (below) is delicious. If you fancy a bit of heat, add a pinch or two of dried red pepper flakes to the peanuts.*

# Cashew Honey Cream

### SERVES 4

⅔ cup raw cashew nuts

1 tablespoon honey

Place the nuts in a small bowl and just cover with cold water. Let soak for 2 hours.

Drain the cashews, reserving the soaking liquid. Place the drained cashews in a small food processor along with 6 tablespoons of the reserved liquid and the honey. Blend for 2–3 minutes, until smooth and creamy, adding extra soaking liquid if needed.

Spoon into a serving bowl, cover with plastic wrap, and chill in the refrigerator until required.

---

# Instant Peanut Butter

### SERVES 6

2 cups salted roasted peanuts

1 tablespoon honey

¼ cup olive or canola oil

Place the peanuts and honey in a food processor and process together for 1 minute.

With the food processor running, add the oil in a steady stream, then blend for another 3–4 minutes, depending on how crunchy or smooth you want it.

Scrape into a sterilized Kilner or other preserving jar or a jam jar, seal, and store in the refrigerator until needed. Will keep in the refrigerator for 2 weeks.

*Spread this thickly onto Meringue Nougats (see page 159) for sandwiching together—it's heavenly! I like to add the brandy, as it makes it truly special. Other options are to spread it on thick toast or simply heat gently and use as a fondue dipping sauce for strawberries and cherries or as a rich chocolate sauce—the hazelnuts can always be omitted. If you want a hint of spice, a pinch of dried red pepper flakes in with the sugar works well.*

# Hazelnut Chocolate Spread

## MAKES ABOUT 1¾ CUPS

1 cup dairy-free light cream

4oz semisweet chocolate, broken into pieces

2 tablespoons superfine sugar

¾ cup whole hazelnuts, toasted and skins rubbed off with a dish towel

1 tablespoon brandy (optional)

Place the cream, chocolate, and sugar in a saucepan over gentle heat and bring to a boil, stirring constantly. Stir in the hazelnuts and brandy, if using.

Pour into a sterilized Kilner or other preserving jar and let cool before sealing. It will keep up to 1 week in the refrigerator.

*Juniper is the perfect match for red cabbage and cranberries. Serve this robust chutney with game such as pheasant or venison, or even with simple sausage and mash.*

# Cranberry, Red Cabbage & Juniper Jam

### SERVES 4–6

2 tablespoons olive oil

2 large red onions, finely sliced

2 cups very finesly shredded red cabbage

1 cup firmly packed light brown sugar

1⅓ cups dried cranberries or dried berry and cherry mix

2 bay leaves

6 juniper berries, crushed

¼ cup balsamic vinegar

1¼ cups red wine

salt and pepper

Heat the oil in a medium saucepan. Add the onions, cover with a lid and cook over medium heat for 10 minutes, until softened.

Add all the remaining ingredients, season with salt and pepper and bring to a boil. Then reduce the heat, replace the lid and simmer for 30 minutes.

Uncover the pan and cook over medium heat for another 10 minutes or until the liquid has reduced to a syrupy consistency.

Serve warm or set to one side to cool before transferring to a sterilized Kilner or other preserving jar or a jam jar and sealing. This will keep for up to 1 week in the refrigerator.

*Roast Tomato Chutney is superb squished onto olive oil toast*
*or as a side for your brunch, picnic, or barbecue. Meltingly soft,*
*the Sweet Pepper Chutney (below) is wonderful as a topping for*
*risottos, pulled through pasta, or dolloped on a homemade burger.*

# Roast Tomato Chutney

## MAKES 1 CUP OR SERVES 4

1lb cherry tomatoes

3 tablespoons olive oil

2 tablespoons balsamic vinegar

2 tablespoons Demerara sugar

2 dried chiles, coarsely broken up

salt and pepper

Preheat the oven to 325°F.

Toss the tomatoes with all the remaining ingredients in a small roasting pan and season to taste with salt and pepper.

Bake for 1¾ hours, until softened and split, but be careful not to let the sugary juices burn on the bottom of the pan—simply add a splash of water if too dry.

Let cool, then transfer to a sterilized Kilner or other preserving jar or a jam jar and seal. The chutney will keep for 3–4 days in the refrigerator.

# Sweet Pepper Chutney

## SERVES 4

3 tablespoons olive oil

2 large red bell peppers, cored, seeded, and finely sliced

2 large orange bell peppers, cored, seeded, and finely sliced

2 bay leaves

3 tablespoons granulated sugar

2 garlic cloves, peeled but kept whole

½ small bunch of soft young thyme, snipped

salt and pepper

Heat the oil in a medium saucepan and stir in the peppers, bay leaves, sugar, garlic cloves, and thyme. Place a piece of wet, crushed wax paper over the pepper mixture and cover with a lid. Cook gently for 35–40 minutes or until the peppers are meltingly soft.

Remove the paper from the pan and increase the heat to reduce the liquid for about 3–4 minutes. Season to taste with salt and pepper.

Let cool, then transfer to a sterilized Kilner or other preserving jar and seal. The chutney will keep for 1 week in the refrigerator.

*Why buy ready-made vinaigrette when you can make it this quickly? Delicious drizzled over a baked potato or spooned over veggies, or simply keep in the refrigerator and use to dress your salads. Serve the Warm Ginger & Orange Sesame Dressing (below) over noodles or spooned over hot rice. This dressing is also great with fresh tuna or strips of steak.*

# Honey, Mustard & Cider Vinaigrette

### SERVES 6

2 tablespoons whole-grain mustard

3 tablespoons cider vinegar

½ cup olive, rapeseed or canola oil

1 tablespoon honey

1–2 tablespoons water

salt and pepper

Place all the ingredients in a sterilized Kilner or other preserving jar. Season well with salt and pepper, seal and shake well.

Store in the refrigerator until needed. Bring to room temperature and shake again before using.

---

# Warm Ginger & Orange Sesame Dressing

### SERVES 4

2 tablespoons sesame seeds

1-inch piece of fresh ginge root, peeled and grated

1 large garlic clove, crushed

1 red chile, seeded and finely chopped

¼ cup sunflower oil

3 tablespoons dark soy sauce

juice of 2 oranges

2 teaspoons sesame oil

salt and pepper

Toast the sesame seeds in a small skillet over medium heat until golden.

Add the ginger, garlic, and chile and cook for 30 seconds. Stir in the remaining ingredients.

Season to taste with salt and pepper and serve warm. Alternatively, set to one side to cool before transferring to a sterilized Kilner or other preserving jar or a jam jar and sealing. This will keep for up to 1 week in the refrigerator.

*This creamy tarragon dressing is great pulled through baby new potatoes, or use it as a delicious dip with French fries or fish goujons. My favorite way to serve the Smoked Pepper Rouille (below) is spooned over a big fish stew or bowl of steamed mussels.*

# Soured Cream & Tarragon Dressing

### SERVES 4

⅔ cup dairy-free light cream

2 teaspoons Dijon mustard

1 tablespoon chopped tarragon leaves

squeeze of lemon juice

salt and pepper

Place all the ingredients in a small bowl and gently mix together.

Season to taste with salt and pepper.

---

# Smoked Pepper Rouille

### SERVES 4–6

2 large red bell peppers

1 tablespoon olive oil

1oz crustless dairy-free white bread, soaked in a little water for 1 minute and excess water squeezed out

2 garlic cloves, crushed

1 teaspoon cayenne pepper

6 tablespoons extra virgin olive oil

salt and pepper

Preheat the oven to 425°F.

Place the peppers on a baking sheet, drizzle over the oil and roast for 35–40 minutes or until the peppers have slightly blackened, turning them occasionally.

Transfer the peppers to a large plastic food bag, seal and let cool.

Remove the peppers from the bag, reserving any of the juices. Peel off the skin, halve and remove the seeds.

Place the pepper flesh in a small food processor with the bread, garlic, cayenne, and the pepper juices and blend until smooth. With the blender or food processor running, slowly drizzle in the extra virgin olive oil. Season to taste with salt and pepper.

*Classic Pesto, the taste of summer! Use both the stems and the leaves of the basil for extra flavor. Walnuts, cashews, and almonds can also be used in place of the traditional pine nuts. As for the Fava Bean & Basil Pistou (below), try serving it on toasted croutes topped with grilled mackerel fillets and a watercress and orange salad. If using fresh fava beans, you may have to skin them unless they are very, very young.*

# Classic Pesto

### SERVES 4

1 small bunch of basil, stems and leaves

1 large garlic clove, crushed

¼ cup pine nuts

⅔ cup olive oil

½ cup finely grated dairy-free sharp cheddar-style cheese

salt and pepper

Wash the basil and add to a small food processor with the water still clinging to it—this will help lighten the pesto. Add the garlic, pine nuts, and oil and blend until thoroughly combined. Be careful not to over-blend—the mixture should be coarse, not smooth and gloopy.

Add the cheese to the food processor and process for a few seconds more. Season well with salt and pepper.

# Fava Bean & Basil Pistou

### SERVES 4–6

2 cups frozen baby fava beans

¼ cup capers, drained

2 garlic cloves, crushed

3 anchovy fillets, drained and torn

1 large bunch of basil

1 cup extra virgin olive oil

salt and pepper

Place the fava beans in a saucepan, cover with boiling water and set aside for 2 minutes. Drain and rinse under cold water. Set aside to drain thoroughly.

Transfer the fava beans to a food processor with the capers, garlic, anchovies, and basil. Pulse in 2-second bursts to form a coarse paste. Trickle in the oil quickly, while pulsing for a few bursts.

Season to taste with pepper and a little salt if needed. Cover and chill until needed. It will keep in the refrigerator for 2–3 days.

*This creamy mayo has a subtle hint of smoked garlic and citrus, and will keep for days in the refrigerator. Don't be tempted to use all olive oil, otherwise it will taste too strong. The speedy, spicy Curry Gravy (below) is great with roasted salmon or pan-fried shrimp, or serve it on the side with roast chicken as a zingy gravy alternative. Try it drizzled in a crusty baked sweet potato topped with juicy shrimp.*

## Smoked Garlic & Chive Mayo

### SERVES 4–6

2 egg yolks

1 teaspoon Dijon mustard

1 teaspoon smoked garlic salt, plus extra to taste if needed

1¼ cups grapeseed oil or a mixture of extra virgin olive oil and grapeseed oil

squeeze of orange juice

2 tablespoons chopped chives

pepper

Place the egg yolks in a bowl with the mustard and smoked garlic salt and beat together.

Gradually beat in half the oil in a slow steady stream. When the mayonnaise starts to become very thick, add the orange juice. Gradually beat in the remaining oil.

Season to taste with pepper, and extra garlic salt if needed, and stir through the chives.

---

## Curry Gravy

### SERVES 4

2 tablespoons Madras curry paste

1 tablespoons tomato paste

1⅔ cups canned coconut milk

squeeze of lemon juice

salt and pepper

Heat a medium saucepan, add the curry paste and tomato paste and cook for 30 seconds.

Add the coconut milk and simmer for 5 minutes. Finish with a squeeze of lemon juice and season to taste with salt and pepper.

*You can't beat homemade chicken stock. You can prepare it as below by poaching a whole chicken or use leftovers from a roast chicken. Either way, it will be full of flavor.*

*A poached chicken may not look very exciting, but boy is it succulent, tasty, and incredibly versatile—just pull away the cooled meat from the carcass, ready for dressing up. Add it to quick, stylish salads, put it over pizza, or use it to make a great chicken pie. For a hearty chowder, simply replace the haddock in the recipe on page 52 with poached chicken pieces.*

# Citrus Chicken Stock Pot

## MAKES ABOUT 2 QUARTS

1 free-range chicken, about 3lb

1 onion, finely sliced

2 carrots, finely sliced

2 celery sticks, finely sliced

3 bay leaves

6 black peppercorns

a few thyme sprigs

2 thick unwaxed lemon slices

Remove the trussing string from the chicken and then pull away any loose fat from the rear end of the bird. Place in a large saucepan or stock pot.

Add all the remaining ingredients to the pan and barely cover with cold water.

Bring to a boil and skim off any fat or scum. Reduce the heat and simmer gently for about 1½ hours, until the chicken is cooked through, making sure that the chicken remains submerged—you may have to weigh it down with a small plate. The legs should feel wobbly and loose when it's ready.

Remove the chicken from the stock and set to one side to cool. Strain the stock, skim off any fat and let cool. Cover and refrigerate until needed.

To store the stock in the freezer, boil the strained stock rapidly until reduced to about 1¾ cups so that it's very concentrated. Let cool, then pour into ice cube trays and freeze. You can then use the frozen cubes as you would a bouillon cube.

*To get the maximum flavor from the root vegetables, make sure you finely slice them all. The addition of herbs and tomato paste gives this stock real oomph.*

# Bouquet Garni Stock

## MAKES ABOUT 5 CUPS

1 tablespoon olive oil

3 celery sticks, finely chopped

1 onion, finely sliced

2 large carrots, finely sliced

2 large thyme sprigs

3 bay leaves

handful of parsley stalks, bruised

2 tablespoons tomato paste

20 black peppercorns

7½ cups cold water

Heat the oil in a large saucepan, add the vegetables and herbs and cook over medium heat for 10 minutes or until golden.

Stir in the tomato paste and cook for 3 minutes.

Add the peppercorns and measured water and bring to a boil, then reduce the heat and simmer gently for 1 hour.

Let cool, then strain, cover and refrigerate until needed.

# Index

# Acknowledgments

*Author's acknowledgments*

Putting a book together is all about team work! Thank you to Stephanie Jackson at Octopus for giving me this opportunity and Alex Stetter, my editor, for all her hard work and patience. Thank you to Jaz Bahra, for the fab layouts and design, to Liz and Max Haarala Hamilton for all the stunningly beautiful photography and to Kat Mead for being such a talent in the kitchen.

Many thanks to my family, Tim, Isaac and Scouty, who chomped their way through this book and are my biggest critics! To Liz Raymont for patiently (and politely) checking and rechecking, always with a smile on her face.

Last but certainly not least, thank you to my sister, Jacks McDonnell Waters, who has always been so dedicated and a total talent to work with. As always, Jacks, such a great pleasure, and I dedicate this book to you, with much love.

*About the author*

Lesley Waters is a regular chef on *Ready Steady Cook*, *Great Food Live*, and *This Morning*, but she is also the former head tutor of Leith's School of Food & Wine, a qualified fitness instructor, and a mother of two. She likes to cook seasonal food whenever possible and her simple, modern style creates recipes that are easy to follow, with stunning results. Teaching has always been Lesley's great passion and opening her own cookery school on the Somerset/Dorset border is the realization of a long-held dream. Her energetic and quirky style of presentation is expertly combined with clear and simple guidance, making her classes both entertaining and informative. Details are available at www.lesleywaters.com

*Dedicated to Jacks McDonnell-Waters*

An Hachette UK Company
www.hachette.co.uk
First published in Great Britain in 2015
by Hamlyn, a division of
Octopus Publishing Group Ltd
Carmelite House
50 Victoria Embankment
London EC4Y 0DZ
www.octopusbooksusa.com

Copyright © Octopus Publishing Group Ltd 2015
Text copyright © Lesley Waters 2015

Distributed in the US by
Hachette Book Group
1290 Avenue of the Americas
4th and 5th Floors
New York, NY 10020

Distributed in Canada by
Canadian Manda Group
664 Annette St. Toronto, Ontario,
Canada M6S 2C8

ISBN 978 0 60063 095 1

Printed and bound in China

10 9 8 7 6 5 4 3 2 1

Publishing Director - Stephanie Jackson
Art Director - Jonathan Christie
Design - Jaz Bahra
Project Editor - Alex Stetter
Illustrations - Abigail Read
Photography - Haarala Hamilton
Home Economist - Kat Mead
Nutritionist - Angela Dowden
Production Controller - Sarah-Jayne Johnson